Radical Notes 4

The Sri Lankan National Crisis and the Search for Solutions

Radical Notes 4

The Sri Lankan National Crisis and the Search for Solutions

S. Sivasegaram

AAKAR

The Sri Lankan National Crisis and the Search for Solutions
S. Sivasegaram

First Published, 2009

ISBN 978-81-89833-85-5

Published by
AAKAR BOOKS
28 E Pocket IV, Mayur Vihar Phase I, Delhi-110 091
Phone : 011-2279 5505 Telefax : 011-2279 5641
aakarbooks@gmail.com; www.aakarbooks.com

Printed at
Arpit Printographers, Delhi-110 032
arpitprinto@yahoo.com

A movement in a sense is a struggle over the definition of reality—how reality is constituted. It is this struggle that builds the focus and targets of the movement, informing the praxes towards social transformation. Inherent in this struggle is the act of reclaiming—sense and sensibility, words and meaning...

The word "radical", which in this post-Cold War phase of Global Capitalism or globaloney has been reduced to a general notion characterizing all kinds of extremism and deviance, is one such word that has been time and again reclaimed by the practitioners of social transformation. "Radical" derived from the Latin word, 'radix' meaning 'root' = 'basic' = 'fundamental' is a concept that aptly defines a transformatory practice as an endeavour to reveal and target the essence of what is given to us in appearance. Radicalism in this sense is nothing but fundamental transformation rather than politicking in appearances. Further, and foremost, it is the all-round critique of the status quo and its genealogies, rather than accepting the disciplinary divide/boundaries that the capitalist system perpetuates in order to control labour-power and labour, our efforts and their fruits.

Radical Notes is an endeavour to coordinate the radical voices around the globe, with special focus on South Asia. In our view such focus (which could have been anything) is not just for convenience, given the facilitators' cultural and intellectual comfort, but is also needed to concretise any 'radical' pursuit. In our view South Asia provides us the opportunity to visualize the reproduction of 'global' capitalism and struggle against it in a regional setting. But we must remember such focus is always fluid with the ever-dynamic radical needs of the humanity.

Radical Notes booklets are contributions on social, cultural, political or economic issues from counter-hegemonic perspectives, which need not be confined to any established socialist and communist current of thought (though these approaches are most welcome).

Series Editors
Radical Notes

Acknowledgments

This book is a revised and updated version of the essay published on the web site http://radicalnotes.com in June 2007. The author is grateful to Pratyush Chandra for encouraging him to write the article and accommodating it in Radical Notes in two parts, in view of its length. The author is grateful to those who previewed the essay and made useful critical comments which were communicated to him through Pratyush. He is also thankful to several of his friends for their useful comments and in particular Dr Soma Arunachalam for his painstaking comments on the text and R Sugunasabesan for his detailed questioning of several points made in the article published by Radical Notes. All of them have helped to improve the contents of the essay. The author is grateful to Radical Notes and Aakar Books for their kindness in coming forward to publish this essay as a book.

S Sivasegaram
December 2008

Contents

1

Introduction

While class contradiction remains the fundamental contradiction in any class society, uneven development of capitalism ensures that class oppression takes different forms so that the struggle against it, to succeed, has to adopt different strategies. Under colonial and semi-colonial domination the struggle was against the main oppressor and emerged as an anti-colonial struggle that united anti-colonial forces while not neglecting contradictions with the local capitalist and feudal classes. Imperialist strategy changed with the elimination of direct colonial rule; and neo-colonialism, while formally recognising the sovereignty of former colonies and semi-colonies, developed methods for direct and indirect control over them. In the process, contradictions that were dormant under colonialism became important issues in countries where a bourgeois elite class replaced the colonial masters.

The absence of a visible foreign oppressor, combined with rivalry among the elite for political power and control over wealth and the need to divert attention from the failure of the new ruling classes to solve the pressing economic problems, enabled contradictions based on identity other than class to come to the fore. When nationalism failed in the face of problems of neo-colonial oppression, the ruling elite encouraged and exploited contradictions based on ethnicity, religion, region and caste, and were often helped in the process by the failings of the left. It is in such a context that the national contradiction came to dominate politics in Sri Lanka. In Sri

Lanka, the aggravation of the national question and its transformation into national oppression and war has made the national question the main contradiction to the extent that, without going some way towards its resolution, it will not be possible to make progress in the anti-imperialist struggle, let alone achieving working class solidarity and carrying forward the struggle for social justice.

The purpose of this essay is to trace the historical development of ethnic and national consciousness in Sri Lanka, the development of the contradictions and their transformation into national conflict, oppression and war; and to identify the respective roles played by ethnicity as well as class interests and ideology. The essay also deals with the different class- and ideology-based approaches to the solution of the national question and touches briefly on the role of forces of foreign domination in aggravating the problem and prescribing solutions that serve their interests.

While the national question is now the main contradiction in Sri Lanka, one needs to be aware that it has been dominated by class interests and that various vested interests have been at play in transforming it into war and in prolonging the war. Although the war is visibly between the armed forces of the Sinhala-dominated Government of Sri Lanka and the Liberation Tigers of Tamil Eelam (LTTE), claiming to represent the entire Tamil nationality, a satisfactory resolution of the national question needs to address other less known contradictions that form part of the national question.

Discussion of the Sri Lankan national question and its manifestation as a war spanning 25 years, with brief lulls, has often been conditioned by subjective interpretations of the problem and its history, and by limited objectives. Subjective interpretations of history, especially but not exclusively by the Sinhala nationalists, have gone a long way towards determining attitudes towards other communities and relationships among nationalities and national minorities. It is also important to recognise the role of class, caste and region in the emergence of ethnic and national identities. The myth of 'purity' of race too has played a role in the consolidation of ethnic identities, and claims largely based on myths concerning who the first settlers in the island are and therefore the 'true sons of the soil' feed chauvinistic attitudes all round.

The resolution of the national question concerns more pressing issues than quarrels relating to ancient history, or for that matter prehistory. Thus, understanding the emergence of ethnic identities over the ages and their consolidation into political categories, and examining how the relationship between the various ethnic groups has been conditioned by socio-economic developments like the introduction of electoral politics under British rule and early rivalries among the elite will help one to appreciate the nature of the problem. Hence the next section will deal with the development of ethnic identities in the context of the relationship between communities and the rivalries among the elite that led to ethnic conflicts. The section that follows it will deal with the national question which had at its centre the contradiction between the Sinhala and Tamil nationalities, leading up to the crisis of 1983. The fourth section provides an overview of the national question from the time that it was transformed into a war up to the current situation, and the fifth section deals with the different approaches to the national crisis and its solution. The final section briefly presents the case for a solution to the national question based on the principle of the right to self-determination applied on the broadest possible basis.

2

The Land and its People: Emerging Ethno-Political Identities

The history of the country and its people cannot be said to be well documented, although historians draw on the *Mahavansa* written around the 5th or 6th century tracing back to the arrival of the exiled mythical Prince Vijaya and his companions from northern India. The chronicle written by *Theravaada* Buddhist clergymen emphasises contradictions with rival schools of Buddhism as well as those with 'alien' Tamils. The historiography of Sri Lanka, with the exception of fairly recent writings by secular modern historians, has been based on the notion that the Sinhalese are the people of the land, Buddhism is their religion, and all else is alien. The claim that the entire Sinhala race, at times referred to as the *Arya Sinhala* race, are the descendents of Vijaya and his companions has been propagated through the ages; and in modern times intensely through both state and private media, and through textbooks. This approach has been a major stumbling block to objective archaeological studies until several decades after independence. But Sinhala historiography is still dominated by subjective interpretations of archaeological data to suit the *Arya Sinhala* myth as well as the Sinhala Buddhist ideology that struck root under British rule in the 19th century. The fallacy of attaching a Sinhala-Buddhist national identity to the ancient feudal state persists despite the fact that many of the kings, including some of the most famed, were not really 'Sinhalese' and had, in addition, South Indian queens who worshipped at Hindu shrines. Hostility between the ethnic groups or for that matter between natives and visitors was if at all minimal, whereas rivalry between Buddhist monasteries for royal favour and between pretenders to the throne for state power had been important causes for disorder.

Sinhala nationalist claims have been contested by Tamil nationalists, who point to the existence of a Tamil kingdom based in the Jaffna peninsula that defied the Portuguese as well as to Tamil principalities and chieftaincies that survived into the British colonial era. References to Saivaite (Hindu) shrines in the island exist in Tamil hymns composed in the 6th-7th century during the Pallava period of South India. More recent excavations point to the existence of the Tamil inscriptions in the northern part of the island dating back to the 3rd century BC. Besides, there is strong evidence that Buddhism thrived among Tamils in the island at least up to the period of Maanikkavaacakar close to 10th century AD, and the *dagobas* unearthed in the north of the island, at least in size, resemble those in Tamilnadu better than the massive structures that are characteristic of Sinhala Buddhism in the South. But to argue therefore that the Tamils of today are the descendents of the ancient Tamils will be as absurd as to claim that the Sinhalese are the descendents of an exiled prince and his companions.

While the possibility of mass scale immigration to the country seems remote, immigration from India, especially South India, has taken place for many centuries under conditions of peace as well as war. Besides two massive South Indian invasions that are said to have dealt deathblows to major Sinhala civilisations, rival kingdoms in the island have throughout history turned to South Indian rulers as well as mercenaries to settle disputes. Also craftsmen and traders entered the island over the centuries, with many of them preserving their identity as individual castes. An examination of Sinhala family names (Tamils did not have a system of family names until the modern era) will show names which are distinctly Tamil and Malayalam that probably date back to not more than a few centuries.

At least two caste groups, namely the Karave (fisher folk)

and Salagama, are known to have South Indian origins going back only a few centuries. The Salagama, most of whom were brought into the island by the Dutch in the 17th and 18th centuries, adopted Sinhala as their language but refused to be identified with the rest of the Sinhala community until as recently as early 20th century. Equally, there have been several foreign settlements among Tamils. When one takes into account the geography of the island that allows easy movement across the land or along the coast and the fact that there was no nation state in the island, which was mostly ruled by rival kings, with parts of the territory under local chieftains, the prospects for inter-racial mixing was high. Also the island, besides continuous interaction with its South Asian neighbours, as well as China during certain periods, has been visited by the Arabs who used it as a trading post for many centuries before the arrival of Europeans.

Thus, while distinct ethnic identities have emerged in the country and have been consolidated and reinforced by socio-political developments, much remains in common between the people and continue to be more than what are used to divide them.

There are four main nationalities in the island: the Sinhalese, Tamils, Muslims and Hill Country Tamils.

The Sinhalese and Sinhala Nationalism. Sinhala identity is based on the mother tongue. However, since the late 19th century the emphasis has shifted to Sinhala Buddhism, so that the Roman Catholic and Protestant Christian Sinhalese are viewed with some suspicion and hostility by extreme Sinhala Buddhist nationalists.

Caste remains an important identifier but its importance has declined in public life; social oppression by caste has been largely eliminated, notably since the formation of the SLFP-led government led by SWRD Bandaranaike in 1956. The decline in the importance of caste was partly due to the access of sizeable sections of caste groups in the coastal areas (earlier ranked low in the caste hierarchy) to modern education, new trades and commercial ventures under colonial rule. Colonial patronage led to the emergence of a land-owning elite class with feudal origins and an emergent merchant capitalist class with feudal links.

Strong differences existed between the Sinhalese of the Hill Country who resisted foreign rule until the fall of Kandyan Kingdom to the British in early 19th century and the Low Country Sinhalese of the coastal region who, from the 16th century, were subject to direct colonial rule by the Portuguese, the Dutch and finally the British owing to various compromises by the rulers with the colonising powers. The first proposal from a Sri Lankan national for federal government came from SWRD Bandaranaike in 1929 during colonial rule, in which he sought separate states for the Kandyan and the Low Country Sinhalese.

The current Sinhala national identity although slow to emerge was guided by Sinhala Buddhist ideology whose foundations were laid in the 19th Century. Its initial targets were the Christian missionaries, both Catholic and Protestant, and in late 19th Century led to localised violence against Catholics at Kochikade about 35 km north of Colombo. The anti-Muslim riot of 1915 was the first instance of widespread violence directed against a community. It was the result of rivalry between the up-and-coming Sinhala Buddhist traders and the already well established Muslim traders. There was also rivalry with South Indian traders who were dominant in some sectors of business, and this rivalry was dealt with by the Citizenship Act, introduced at the time of independence in 1948 to deprive an entire ethnic group, mainly comprising plantation workers, of their right to citizenship.

Sinhala chauvinism developed adherents among the petit bourgeoisie. The right-wing trade unionist AE Goonesinghe, a pioneer leader of the trade union movement in the country, targeted the strong Malayali working class community based in Colombo that played a major role in building the left-wing trade union movement, and in particular that affiliated to the Communist Party.

The Tamil elite with a feudal background was conservative in its thinking. Although some of the Tamils who settled in Colombo were successful in business, and acquired considerable wealth, Tamils (meaning here Ceylon Tamils as they were known then, with roots in the Northern and Eastern Provinces) were not serious rivals to the Sinhalese in the business sector to be seen as a threat by the Sinhala business community. Rivalry with Tamils largely concerned middle class aspirations. A resolution was introduced in the State Council in 1943 to replace English with Sinhala as the official language, by JR Jayawardane who was to be a founder member of the United National Party (UNP) formed on the eve of national independence. Although it was deflected by consensus to make Tamil also an official language, the resolution was a clear indicator of what lay ahead for the Tamil middle classes whose presence was strong among white collar government employees. The advantage that the Tamils had in state employment was because of the setting up of Christian missionary schools in the Jaffna peninsula which gave a head start for the Tamil elite as well as middle classes, while not doing much to knock down caste barriers. Making Sinhala the sole official language on 1956 was rightly seen by the Tamil leaders as an act of discrimination against Tamils. That was to be followed in the decades to come by blatant discrimination against the Tamils in education, employment and various other fields.

Sinhala nationalism developed in the course of aggressive expansion of the emergent Sinhala capitalist class and the consolidation of political power in the hands of an elite group with feudal origins and loyalty to the British colonial masters.

Tamil identity and Tamil nationalism. The term 'Tamil nationality' generally refers to Tamils (once known as 'Ceylon Tamils') from the Northern and Eastern Provinces, and excludes the Muslims and Hill Country Tamils.

Tamil awareness based on linguistic identity was subject to various constraints and slow to emerge. Tamil Saivaite (also referred to as Tamil Hindu) revivalism in the latter part of the 19th century arose in response to Protestant Christian proselytising in the North, which took advantage of missionary control of modern school education and thereby access to the professions and state employment. Notably, conversion to

Protestant Christianity was not in response to caste oppression but for socio-economic advantage, and attracted mainly the upper caste middle classes forming the core of the caste-conscious Tamil community of the North. Tamil Saivaite revivalism, like its Sinhala Buddhist counterpart, was not anti-colonial, but anti-Christian.

A class of traders in agricultural produce, tobacco in particular, emerged under British rule and traded in the South as well as in South India. Some of the more successful sections of the Tamil elite invested in education and in property in the South, mainly Colombo, to become the Colombo-based Tamil elite whose members dominated politics in the early part of the 20th century.

Given the predominance of the Vellala caste in the North and the exclusion of the depressed castes from access to education and opportunity for social advancement, the Jaffna-centred Tamil politics initially emphasised Tamil Vellala Saivaite interests, and in course of time accommodated Vellala Christians. This leadership, based in Colombo, was insensitive to the aspirations of Tamil masses living outside its power base in the Jaffna peninsula. With caste divisions running deep and caste oppression more severe than elsewhere in the island, the emergence of a Tamil national identity had to wait until this elite group was confronted by Sinhala-Buddhist chauvinism.

The prospect of sharing the spoils with the colonial master implied rivalry among the elite groups. The nature of the rivalry became more clearly on ethnic lines following the move towards elected government, and universal franchise soon after. It is, however, remarkable that Tamils in the North were the first to articulate progressive political thought: a sizeable section of the educated Tamil middle classes and an enlightened section of the elite, inspired by the Indian independence movement and leaders like Gandhi and Nehru, formed the Jaffna Youth Congress which was the first organisation in the country to call for independence from British colonial rule. (It was the left movement of the country that carried that campaign forward, but a combination of circumstances ensured that Sri Lanka had no independence struggle comparable with those in other Asian colonies of the time). The Youth Congress also defied the conservative elite in standing by the women and the depressed castes to call for universal franchise. Thus, despite awareness of Tamil ethnic identity, the Tamil leadership of the time thought in terms of the whole country so that a Tamil nation and secession were not serious political considerations, although betrayal by their Sinhala elite counterparts led the prominent Tamil political leaders P Arunachalam and P Ramanathan to found Tamil political organisations in the 1920s.

Sinhala nationalism, or rather Sinhala-Buddhist ideology, became increasingly assertive in the run up to independence, and it was against this background that Tamil parliamentary political parties emerged. The All Ceylon Tamil Congress (ACTC), the main Tamil political party of the time, and other Tamil leaders were willing to barter their support for the Sinhala nationalist UNP in exchange for cabinet posts and other favours. Class interests ensured that this love-hate relationship survived several tests.

The Tamil leaders were offended by the design of the national flag, which implied Sinhala pre-eminence. Colonisation schemes, conceived in the post World War II years before independence and implemented since the early 1950s in the Eastern Province, aimed at taking away fertile land from Tamils and Muslims and settling Sinhalese there and thereby reduce the Tamils and Muslims to a minority in their traditional homeland, did not pass unnoticed, but did not lead to a struggle at the time. The Citizenship Act which deprived the Hill Country Tamils (then known as Indian Tamils) was supported by several Tamil MPs for various inducements offered by the UNP leadership, but was opposed by the entire left. The dubious role played by the ACTC leadership in this issue split the ACTC and led to the founding of the Federal Party (FP) in 1949.

The FP claimed to speak for all the Tamil-speaking people (including the Muslims and Hill Country Tamils) and sought a federal form of government with the Northern and Eastern Provinces constituting a federal state for the Tamil-speaking people and the rest of the country a predominantly Sinhala state.

The kind of federal solution proposed by the FP showed a lack of vision since it was inadequate to address the problems faced by the Muslims who were distributed throughout the island with pockets of large concentrations in the East and a few on the west coast of the island. The FP demanded the restoration of citizenship to the Hill Country Tamils, but abandoned the Hill Country Tamils to the putative Sinhala dominated federal state. Nevertheless, it was the FP that gave form to the concept of Tamil national identity. But it took until the 'Sinhala Only' cry of 1956 for the FP to establish itself as the main Tamil party.

The concept of 'Tamil-speaking people' alone was inadequate to unite the three ethnic groups against oppression by Sinhala nationalism. The FP, which in reality only represented the Tamils ('Ceylon Tamils'), by addressing the national question as one concerning a Sinhala-speaking majority and a Tamil-speaking minority, failed not only to take into account the fact that each of the three 'Tamil-speaking' ethnic groups had developed separate identities but also to appreciate the complex socio-economic and political circumstances under which it happened. And the just demand of the Tamils for their rights suffered the consequences of this folly in the decades to come.

Muslims: Religion as Ethnic Marker. The Sri Lankan Muslim community is predominantly Tamil-speaking, but has maintained an identity distinct from that of the Tamils for many reasons. Importantly, the community is scattered throughout the country with a majority living in the predominantly Sinhala South. While the claim by some Muslim leaders that they are descendants of Arab settlers in Sri Lanka is questionable, it is true that a significant number have Arab ancestors. The argument that the Muslims adopted Tamil as their language merely because it was the language of commerce in the region will not apply to most Muslims. The desire for the community to hold together and the presence of a sizeable number of Muslims of South Indian origin could have played an important part in the choice of a common language. However, the Muslims have lived in relative harmony with their Sinhalese and Tamil neighbours until the emergence of Sinhala and Tamil nationalist politics.

The importance that the Muslims attach to their linguistic identity varies with class and geographic location. However, the religious identity, besides taking precedence over the linguistic, has become very assertive within the community.

At the time of independence there was a considerably large Tamil-speaking 'Indian Muslim' community besides other Muslim communities of Indian origin. The population of these communities, especially the 'Indian Muslims', has shrunk since independence for a variety of reasons; and while these communities still preserve their identity within the Muslim nationality, they increasingly tend to identify themselves publicly as Muslims.

Among subjective factors that contributed to the Muslims insisting on an identity distinct from the Tamils are the tendency for certain Tamil nationalist leaders to claim that the Muslims are Tamils who had converted to Islam, and memories of the anti-Muslim violence of 1915, when a very prominent Tamil leader sided with the Sinhala-Buddhist chauvinists at whose hands the Muslims had suffered. Considerations of survival made it necessary for the Muslims to adapt to their environment, and efforts by the Tamil nationalist leadership to count them among Tamils while not addressing problems specific to them drove the Muslims further away from an identity based on language. Muslim attitudes were further hardened by hostile acts by the Tamil militant movements since the mid-1980s.

Although the Muslims have for long asserted in various ways their identity as a nationality distinct from the Tamils, there was no claim to nationhood until the mid-1980s. The notion of a 'Muslim nation' has been actively promoted by a section of the Muslims from the East since the early-1990s, but has failed to attract mass support, although the creation of one or several Muslim autonomous units in regions with large Muslim concentrations had broad appeal among the Muslims.

It should also be noted here that a lack of facilities in much of the South to learn in the Tamil medium, the hope of better career prospects by learning in the Sinhala medium, and persuasion by a section of the Southern Muslim leadership have tempted an increasing number of Muslims, especially from the middle classes in the South, to have their children educated in the Sinhala medium. The evolution of a Sinhala-speaking Muslim community with little knowledge of Tamil would, however, have serious implications for the unity of the Muslims as a nationality.

Hill Country Tamils. The term Hill Country Tamils refers to the descendents of people who were brought into the country in the 19th century by the British, mostly as indentured labour and employed predominantly in the tea and, later, rubber plantations. They were deprived of their citizenship and the right to vote in 1948 and, under the 'Sirima-Shastri Pact' of 1964, India agreed to the 'repatriation' of some 525,000 individuals to India while Sri Lanka would grant citizenship to 300,000, and the fate of the rest (estimated at 150,000) would be determined later. This harsh decision was denounced by the genuine left (but not by the parliamentary left parties) since the Pact failed to consider the views of the people affected by it, a vast majority of whom would have preferred Sri Lankan citizenship. The agreement, to be implemented within a 15-year time frame, was slow to take effect for political and practical reasons.

The plantation workers are still the lowest-paid wage labourers in the country with a normal daily wage that is less than half that for casual unskilled labour in urban areas. The nationalisation of the plantations in 1972 under land reform legislation, falsely hailed by the parliamentary left as a socialist measure, led to Sinhala nationalists taking control of the plantations at various managerial levels. This added to the misery to the plantation workers. Some tea estates were closed, the workers expelled, and the land distributed to Sinhalese villagers for political gain. The drought conditions that followed in 1973-75 led to a shortage of working days. This combination of circumstances drove a sizeable section of the plantation workers out of the tea estates and a considerable number were reduced to begging on the streets. Those who moved to the North in search of agricultural and farm work found that life was no better under Tamil employers. Attempts by humane

Tamil nationalists to settle the Hill Country Tamils in the North and the East had limited success owing to difficulties created by the state. The deteriorating living conditions in the plantations, escalating ethnic tensions since 1977, and the violence against the Hill Country Tamils in 1980 and 1983 led, in the decade since 1975, to the 'repatriation' of around four hundred thousand Hill Country Tamils to India, a land where none of them had ever set foot before.

The term Indian Tamil was used to refer to them until the 1960s in view of their relatively recent Indian origin compared to the Sinhala and (Ceylon) Tamil nationalities. The Hill Country Tamils are predominantly members of the working class employed in the tea and rubber plantations; a smaller section is employed in other sectors in different parts of the country. There is a sizeable middle class comprising middle-level managers, small traders and a slowly growing class of urban white-collar workers. The term Hill Country Tamils has since replaced the term Indian Tamils, to emphasise a sense of belonging to Sri Lanka and not India.

Wealthy members of the community resent the term Hill Country Tamils in view of its association with the plantations and the implied class connotations; and recent attempts to re-label the community as "Tamils of Indian Origin" failed as a result of the rise in political consciousness of the Hill Country Tamils and their assertion of their identity as a distinct nationality. Political consciousness was slow to arrive owing to the educational backwardness of the community and the systematic denial of educational opportunities by the plantation management, which also ensured that, at least in the tea estates where most of them lived, the Tamil-speaking workers did not interact with the Sinhalese from villages neighbouring the estates. Hostility thus existed between the plantation workers and poor and landless Sinhalese peasants in parts of the central highlands, where the peasantry saw the plantation workers as alien occupiers of land which could have been lawfully theirs. This hostility suited both the Sinhala exploiting classes and the Hill Country Tamil elite that dominated the trade unions in the plantations, since it prevented the coming together of two severely oppressed sections of the population. There was also resentment among Hill Country Tamils about exploitation by the 'high-caste' middle-class Tamils, mainly from the North, working as teachers and officials from British colonial times and well into the 1960s.

Although ethnic consciousness among Hill Country Tamils developed in response Sinhala chauvinism and exploitation by middle-class Tamils from the North, political consciousness, hindered by the disenfranchisement in 1948, was slow to develop. While the reactionary elite of the Ceylon Workers' Congress (CWC), the predominant trade union cum political party in the tea plantations, took advantage of the 'Indian' label to keep unionised labour in its control, the poor educational background of the workers and the restrictive practices of the plantation management stood in the way of progressive politics.

Hard work by educationalists from the community, leftists, and progressive trade unionists enabled the emergence of a sizeable population of politically conscious educated youth and to greater awareness of the rights among the people. A series of mass struggles led in stages to the eventual restoration of citizenship to all Hill Country Tamils near the end of the last millennium, further consolidating the status of Hill Country Tamils as a distinct nationality. Meanwhile the Hill Country Tamils face increased threats from forces of Sinhala chauvinism seeking to weaken them politically by a process of Sinhala colonisation and forced displacement of the Hill Country Tamils from areas where they live in large numbers.

Besides the four nationalities, there are several national minorities that have historically asserted their individuality. The following are important.

Burghers. The term refers to descendents of the Portuguese and Dutch settlers in the Island. The Portuguese settled in larger numbers than the Dutch and there has been considerable mixing with the local population. Within the Burgher community, which is entirely urban and predominantly English-speaking, there is a sharp distinction between the Portuguese descendents who are almost exclusively Roman Catholics and the descendents of the Dutch, a majority of whom belong to the

Dutch Reformed Church. The numerically smaller Burgher community living among Tamils of the North and East uses Tamil for its day-to-day activities and, until recently, had a sizeable number of speakers of a Portuguese Creole.

The Burgher community outside the North and East, although culturally European-oriented, was well integrated with the local communities, had a strong sense of belonging, and actively participated in national politics. Notably, some remarkable works on the history, culture, geography and the flora and the fauna of the country were by eminent members of the Burgher community.

The rise of Sinhala-Buddhism and the animosity of the Sinhala nationalists towards the Burgher community worried it so that, following the passage of the Official Language Act (better known as the 'Sinhala Only' Act) in 1956, a majority, from among the lighter skinned English-speaking sections, took advantage of the immigration policy of the Australian government giving preference to European descendents, to migrate to Australia in large numbers. The remaining members still retain their ethnic identity as Burghers, but are less assertive in the political affairs of the country.

Malays. The community comprises descendents of people from Java, brought into the island by the Dutch colonial masters who also controlled Indonesia, and ethnic Malays who arrived later during British rule from Malaya (now the most populous part of Malaysia). Several prominent political and social leaders came from the community which asserted its distinctness from the Muslims (then referred to as Ceylon and Indian Moors).

A combination of circumstances, including the marginalisation of the community in sectors of employment like the armed forces and the police, where earlier there was significant Malay presence, and the rise of Muslim nationalism, has politically weakened the Malays. Despite alignment with mainstream Muslim politics, the Malays are still assertive of their social and cultural identity as distinct from that of the Muslim nationality.

Attho. The plight of the aboriginals of this country is comparable with that of many native communities in the

Americas and Australia. The Attho, numbering around 4500, have preserved the basic features of the aboriginal community for over 2500 years and live mainly in the forests of the Mahiyangana region of the Uva Province, and make their livelihood as hunter-gatherers and *chena* (slash and burn) cultivators. Their territory has gradually shrunk as a result of systematic encroachment in the name of development, by the state as well as by capitalist predators. The Attho have their own language, which probably has a longer history in the island than either Sinhala or Tamil. Their system of worship, customs and cultural traditions are distinct from those of the Sinhalese and Tamils, although there has always been interaction between the Attho and the Sinhalese and Tamils in adjoining regions.

The community, while finding it increasingly hard to make a living in the traditional way, is not given the opportunity to modernise on its own terms. Meanwhile, there is, with state support, social and political pressure on the Attho to abandon their way of life and thereby assimilate it to Sinhala Buddhist identity.

Other Muslim communities: Special mention must be made of communities such as the Borah, and Memens, who are considered part of the Muslim nationality, since they have distinct ethnic roots and cultural features and assert their individuality to resist integration with the Sri Lankan Muslims. Indian Muslims, who were once distinguished from their Sri Lankan Counterparts by the terms Ceylon Moor and Indian Moor, have dwindled in number. Given their cultural proximity to the Sri Lankan Muslims, they could in course of time integrate with the latter.

Other Communities with Tamil Identity. Immigrant communities from South India such as the Colombo Chetties and the Parava who settled mainly along the west coast have kept their Tamil linguistic identity but have always asserted their respective identities as distinct from that of the Tamils. The term Indian Tamils refers to people of Indian nationality living in Sri Lanka as well as to naturalised Indian Tamils. They are mostly members of business communities and are reluctant to be identified with the other Tamil nationalities.

Excluded Sinhala Communities. Two Sinhala-speaking communities with a long history, namely the Rodi, a community of outcastes, and the Gypsies, are not integrated with the Sinhala society. Both communities have been historically discriminated against and viewed with a mix of suspicion, fear and contempt.

Malayalis. Although the Malayalis have ceased to be a distinct ethnic group in Sri Lanka, they, despite being a community of immigrant workers, made a positive impact on the political affairs of the island. They identified closely with the people of this country and contributed to the winning of trade union and political rights. The leading role of the vibrant Malayali immigrant community of workers and intelligentsia in the early part of the 20th century in the left and trade union movements met with the wrath of Sinhala chauvinism in the 1930s, which led to the elimination of the Malayali ethnic identity. A good number of them stayed back even after independence, of whom a majority returned to Kerala by 1960, and those who remained have integrated themselves with the Sinhala and Tamil nationalities.

The foregoing identifies the role of Sinhala Buddhist chauvinism in marginalising ethnic minorities from the various sectors of social activity in the country. It also identifies how narrow nationalism grew in response to chauvinism and the role of class in the emergence of nationalist and ethnic politics. Thus, even before independence from colonial rule, signs had emerged that, without the predominance of working-class politics, the national question would take centre stage in the politics of the island.

3

The National Question Becomes the Main Contradiction

The Run-up to the Sea Change of 1956. As stated earlier, there was no independence struggle in Sri Lanka (then Ceylon). In 1948, the British colonial masters transferred power to a loyal section of the Sinhala nationalist elite who dominated the United National Party (UNP) founded in 1947. The unitary form of government as set out in the constitution, despite built-in safeguards against legislation inimical to the minority communities, failed at its first hurdle with the disenfranchisement of the Hill Country Tamils. The parliamentary system, which was to become a tyranny in the name of the majority, offered no possibility of redress for this injustice. Given the conservative elitist leadership of the CWC representing the plantation workers, the indifference of the ACTC, and a majority of the Tamil MPs who had become part of the government, the campaign against the legislation fizzled out.

Although the Muslims were the first target of Sinhala-Buddhist chauvinism because of business rivalries early in the 20th century and the Malayalis in the 1930s for anti-left political reasons, with the Hill Country Tamils politically disarmed in 1948, the Tamil community became the main target of Sinhala chauvinism in the 1950s. The predominance of Tamils in a large and contiguous territory, their claim to a long history in the island, and the challenge posed by the Tamil leadership to Sinhala dominance were major considerations. However, the emergence of a new generation of educated middle classes Sinhalese vying with the Tamils for government jobs and other white collar employment was of greater electoral significance than matters that directly concerned bourgeois and feudal elite interests.

The Tamil leadership was conscious of the intentions of the Sinhala chauvinist leadership so that the ACTC had proposed an alternative formula for parliamentary representation in independent Sri Lanka that would avert a Sinhala-dominated government with absolute power. But the way in which the proposal was structured failed to gain support from other minority communities and was rejected. Despite its own approach being based on parliamentary political strategy, the FP, formed in 1949, saw the flaw in the collaborationist approach of the ACTC, and warned the Tamils that what befell the Hill Country Tamils would soon befall them. The FP demanded a federal form of government that would safeguard the interests of the 'Tamil-speaking people' as a whole, but failed to convince the Jaffna Tamil electorate at the polls in 1952, and was badly defeated by the ACTC.

The fortunes of the FP changed with the adoption of the 'Sinhala Only' language policy by both the UNP and the Sri Lanka Freedom Party (SLFP, founded in 1951 by UNP dissenters led by SWRD Bandaranaike) in the run up to the general election in 1956; the FP was to dominate Tamil politics from that time until Tamil militants posed a challenge from around 1980. The FP in 1956 put forward as its four demands, granting Tamil parity of status with Sinhala as official language, setting up of a federal form of government to address the concerns of the Tamil-speaking people, stopping state-sponsored colonisation of Sinhalese in predominantly Tamil-speaking areas, and granting citizenship to all Hill Country Tamils. While these were just demands, the emphasis of the FP was on the language problem which affected a sizeable section of the Tamil middle class which depended on government service for its livelihood, but not the Muslims and the Hill Country Tamils to the same extent.

Bandaranaike successfully rallied around the SLFP an assortment of the petit bourgeois classes, and capitalised on mass resentment of the UNP for its policies that failed to address the needs of the common masses as well as its brutal handling of the *Hartal* of 1953. Although Bandaranaike, who was not literate in Sinhala, came from a Sinhala Christian elite family and converted to Buddhism for political advantage, his opportunist pledge to make Sinhala the official language had greater credibility than a similar pledge by the UNP which had ruled the country in English for eight years. The pledge, besides stirring up Sinhala nationalist sentiments, had mass appeal for practical reasons: it appealed to the Sinhala educated youth aspiring for government employment and addressed the resentment of the ordinary people who could not get anything done in government offices in their language and had to seek the help of someone who knew English. Thus the Sinhala Only policy was a populist move with Sinhala chauvinist as well as anti-imperialist connotations. The electoral success in 1956 of the SLFP-led alliance including the Trotskyite VLSSP of Philip Gunawardane as well as various minor chauvinistic parties, under the banner of Mahajana Eksath Peramuna (MEP, a name that Gunawardane was to take over after the break-up of the alliance in 1959), also marked for the Sinhala masses an upsurge in national awareness and, for the first time, a sense of belonging in the affairs of the state.

The left (this time with the exception of the VLSSP which was in the MEP coalition) joined the Tamil MPs and the Muslim MPs from the East to oppose the Official Language Act making Sinhala the sole official language. Muslim MPs from the South who either belonged to the SLFP or to the UNP voted with their parties in favour of the Act.

The Tamil Response and Consequences. The response of the Tamil leadership, especially the FP, to the Official Language Act was rash. The FP organised a massive rally in Trincomalee in the same year that the Act was passed in parliament to demand parity of status for Tamil, but with no plans for a mass struggle. It appealed to Tamil government servants not to learn Sinhala even if it meant losing their jobs, and canvassed Tamil schools in the North to cease teaching Sinhala as an optional subject.

Realising the strength of feeling among the Tamils, Bandaranaike entered into an agreement (known as the Banda-Chelva Pact) with Chelvanayakam, the leader of the FP, that went some way towards accommodating the three of the four demands of the FP that pertained to the Tamils of the North and East, through the setting up of District Councils with considerable autonomy including a major say in colonisation schemes, and provisions for the use of Tamil for official purposes, while retaining Sinhala as the official language. The Left fully supported the agreement, but Bandaranaike, when confronted by a section of the Sinhala chauvinistic Buddhist clergy with whose support he came to power in 1956, yielded to their threats and tore up the agreement.

What served as the pretext for tearing up the agreement was the campaign launched by the FP in January 1958 to replace the Sinhala character reading 'Sri' from motor vehicle number plates with its Tamil equivalent. The introduction of the character 'Sri' in late 1957 to replace the existing English letter series was a gesture to please Sinhala chauvinists. The over-reaction of the FP to make it a campaign issue led to Sinhala chauvinists blacking out Tamil letters in name boards of shops, streets etc. and culminated in the first major anti-Tamil violence of May 1958. (There were, however, several incidents of attacks on Tamils in the wake of the passage of the Sinhala Only Act in 1956 but rather sporadic and much smaller in scale). The government failed to act until after the killing of several hundred Tamils and many more incidents of rape, assault, arson and looting. Rather than bring to book the culprits, the government placed under house arrest a few Sinhala extremist politicians and, to placate Sinhala chauvinist sentiments, detained all the MPs from the FP.

In August 1958, the government passed legislation to enable the use of Tamil for a number of specified official purposes. But the provisions of the Act were rarely implemented because of wilful indifference of the government and officials in key administrative positions.

The Continuing Pattern. The pattern of events recurred with increased impact until the anti-Tamil pogrom of 1983 July.

Major events that offended Tamil sentiments between 1958 and 1970 and the response of the Tamil leadership are summarised in the paragraphs below. They led to further deterioration of the relationship between the two communities to make the national question the main contradiction.

In 1960 the SLFP government made Sinhala the official language for litigation by the Language of the Courts Act. Negotiations between the government and the FP made slow progress, and in 1961 the FP, with little preparation, decided to launch a Satyagraha campaign, based on Gandhian principles, for the language rights of the Tamils. Police brutality against demonstrators led to mass support for the campaign, the aims of which were supported by the left, although the Communist Party was critical of the approach of the FP. The *faux pas* by the FP in printing postal stamps for a putative Tamil federal state provided the pretext for the government to slap down a state of emergency and the campaign came to a grinding halt. Rather than address the just grievances of the Tamils, the government began in 1961 to implement in earnest the official language legislation.

The leaders of the FP, who were released from detention after several months, launched another poorly organised campaign in 1962 to persuade the Tamil people to carry out all correspondence with the government in Tamil. The campaign failed to take off since it was the upper stratum of the Tamil community, which was more at ease in English, which corresponded most with government. A campaign to persuade Tamils to settle in new land development schemes in the East around the same time too failed to take off because of the reluctance of the Tamils in Jaffna to leave the peninsula. (This was, however, to change in the 1970s when agriculture became a profitable venture owing to a restriction on the import of several food items). Efforts of the FP for legal redress through litigation by its clerical service trade union also proved futile.

Despite the populist approach of the FP in the 1950s and the public enthusiasm for it up to the *Satyagraha* of 1961, the FP had by 1962 shown beyond reasonable doubt that it was not a force capable of leading the Tamil people into struggle for their rights. It was thus condemned to tread a path no different from that of the ACTC between 1948 and 1956.

In the general election of 1965 the FP openly sided with the UNP based on an agreement between the leaders of the two parties Chelvanayakam and Dudley Senanayake and known as the Dudley-Chelva Pact, and became a partner in the UNP-led government which also included Sinhala extremist parties. Regulations for the use of the Tamil language enacted in 1966, under the Tamil Language (Special Provisions) Act of 1958, met with protests not only from the SLFP but also the LSSP and the CP, each of which had undergone a split in 1964. The revolutionary factions of the LSSP and the CP denounced the opportunism of the parliamentary left. The Regulations, like the legislation of 1958, failed to be implemented. Unable to make progress in setting up District Councils as set out in the Dudley-Chelva Pact, the FP left the government in 1968 on a weaker pretext, but continued its close ties with the UNP and support for the government.

An Electoral Shock. An SLFP-led coalition with the LSSP and CP, called the United Front (UF) swept to power in 1970 to form the government, to the dismay of the FP which boasted in 1960 and 1965 that the Tamils will be the deciding force in determining who forms the government in the country. Distrust between the FP and the UF worsened with time for a variety of reasons.

On suspicion that Tamil examiners were over-marking Tamil medium answer scripts at the GCE(AL) examination of 1970, based on which the university admissions were to be decided, a system of media-wise 'standardisation' of the raw marks was introduced. This drastically reduced the eligibility of Tamil students to university admission, especially in the sciences and professional degree programmes. Although a government inquiry ruled that there was no malpractice, standardisation continued until 1974, when a 'district quota' system was introduced, that benefited Tamil and Muslim students from educationally backward districts outside Jaffna, but kept low the overall percentage of Tamil-medium admissions. Given the dependence of the Tamil middle classes on government jobs and the professions, standardisation aroused feelings of resentment among the educated middle class Tamil youth of the North, and the seeds of militancy were sown.

The JVP Shows its Fangs. Meanwhile, the Sinhala nationalist Janatha Vimukthi Peramuna (JVP), with Marxist pretences, launched its adventurist insurrection in April 1971. At the time the JVP was not overtly hostile to the Tamils, but portrayed the Hill Country Tamils as arms of 'Indian expansionism', as they understood the term, and went to the extent of wanting to rid the country of Hill Country Tamils. Its armed struggle against the state, although disastrous, had an impact on Tamil militancy in the North, which had already witnessed a successful armed action led by Marxist Leninists against caste oppression between 1966 and 1971.

The Parliamentary Left Surrenders to Chauvinism. The constitution of 1972 was drafted by Colvin R de Silva a veteran Trotskyite who once suggested the demolition of a famous dagoba and the use of the bricks to build public toilets, and best remembered for his famous quote, "Two languages, one country. One language, two countries" in 1956. The constitution by which the country changed its name from Ceylon to Sri Lanka and declared itself a republic so that the monarch of Britain ceased to be the formal head of state, also disposed of the earlier constitutional safeguards against legislation oppressive to minority ethnic groups and made it the duty of the state 'to protect Buddhism'. The FP, which withdrew from the Constituent Assembly (CA) set up in 1970 in protest against the refusal by the CA to consider its draft proposals, denounced the Constitution, which was also strongly criticised by Marxist Leninists and Trotskyite groups that rejected the parliamentary path to socialism.

The escalation of the antagonism of the FP towards the government was to a considerable extent due to the UF government acting in various ways to undermine the standing of the FP among Tamils. But the FP compounded the problem by aligning itself more closely with the UNP and encouraging Tamil militancy. (Encouragement of Tamil militancy has been attributed to A Amirthalingam, a leading member of the FP, who has been accused of using the disgruntled Tamil youth to rebuild his authority in the FP, following his loss of parliamentary seat amid the electoral success of the FP in 1970, but with a decline for the first time in its share of votes).

The Drift towards Tamil Eelam. The FP decided to bury the hatchet with its rival, the ACTC to form a Tamil United Front (TUF) in 1972 to fight for the rights of the Tamils that have been denied by the new constitution. The partners, besides the FP and the ACTC, interestingly, included the CWC, whose leader S Thondaman was a nominated MP in the earlier UNP-led government but sidelined by the UF, and KW Devanayagam a prominent Tamil MP and UNP politician from the East. The TUF proved inadequate to address the escalating unrest among the Tamil youth caused by the growing frustration with the continuing discrimination in education and employment among other things and the heavy handed approach of the government in dealing with the militant youth.

The dispute over the venue for the Fourth International Tamil Research Conference in January 1974, the clumsy handling of visas for participants by the government and the desire of the FP to transform the event into political theatre to force a confrontation with the police culminated in the insensitive conduct of the police that led to the killing of nine people in a stampede, for which the government failed to take responsibility or act to bring the offenders to book. This added fuel to the fury of young Tamil militants already angered by standardisation. There were attempts on the life of Alfred Duraiappah, the SLFP Organiser for Jaffna, who was once an MP for Jaffna and a popular former Mayor of Jaffna. The subsequent killing of Duraiappah in 1975 July marked the start of a cycle of violence involving the Tamil militants and the police as well as a series of political assassinations of 'Tamil traitors', with the blessings of some TUF leaders, subsequently extended to rival militants as well as the leaders themselves.

The Tamil United Liberation Front (TULF) evolved from the TUF in 1976, with the FP and a section of the ACTC as main constituents, and declared as its goal a separate state of Tamil

Eelam. But it is doubted to this day if the TULF really meant it: a much spoken of public debate in 1975 between the revolutionary Communist Party leader N Sanmugathasan and the FP parliamentarian V Tharmalingam and a subsequent series of debates on the subject involving the two parties revealed that the TULF had no plan whatsoever to achieve its declared goal of Tamil Eelam. The TULF overcame the problem by prohibiting its members from public debates on the subject. The events that followed 1977 showed that Tamil Eelam was only a ploy to placate the disgruntled youth and deter them from militant activities and a means of reversing the declining electoral fortunes of the FP and ACTC.

Calling the TULF Bluff. The UNP, whose leader JR Jayawardane had an understanding with the TULF and the CWC, scored an unprecedented victory at the elections of 1977, bagging 5/6 of all seats in Parliament, with the SLFP reduced to a mere 8 seats out of a total of around 150 seats, and the parliamentary left, which contested separately following the break-up of the UF, suffering absolute humiliation at the polls. The leader of the TULF, Amirthalingam, was content with his new role as Leader of the Opposition in the hope that Jayawardane would deliver on his promises. Jayawardane delivered on his promise of increasing the proportion of the students admitted on merit, a matter in which the Sinhala elite too had an interest, but had no intention of dealing with the more serious grievances of the Tamils. Instead he sought to put the Tamils 'in their place'. The anti-Tamil violence that broke out in 1977 only weeks after the elections surpassed the events of 1958 and was the worst act of mass crime since the arrival of European colonialists in 1505, until the pogrom of 1983. In 1980 the Hill Country Tamils faced the first spate of mob violence against them on a mass scale, although localised violence existed and was on the rise since the nationalisation of the plantations in 1973.

The Constitution of 1978 made JR Jayawardane Executive President, and he supplemented his almost dictatorial powers with other dubious methods of political control. The constitution, however, made some concessions to the language demands of the Tamils, twenty-two years too late but not intended to be implemented, while it had provisions that militated against the interests of the Tamils, namely granting Buddhism foremost place and making Sinhala the language of administration.

Rising Militancy and the Fall of the TULF. By 1978 the TULF had started to lose its credibility with the Tamil electorate, and dissidents began to assert themselves. The UNP government passed legislation banning the Liberation Tigers of Tamil Eelam in May 1978 and followed it with the draconian Prevention of Terrorism Act of July 1979. In a desperate bid for survival, the TULF leadership gambled what was left of its credibility by placing its trust in the political brokerage of AJ Wilson, an unashamed supporter of the UNP and son-in-law of the late Chelvanayakam, the much adored leader of the FP. After two years of wrangling Wilson extracted from Jayawardane in 1980 the District Development Councils Act. The DDCs were so pathetic that they had even less authority and resources than a local authority; and the government rubbed salt into the wound by its blatant malpractices during the elections to the Jaffna DDC in 1981, and topped it up with burning down the Jaffna Library, one of the finest libraries in South Asia.

It was after that the TULF flirted with the idea of doing business with the 'parliamentary left' to mobilise resistance to the corrupt and authoritative UNP regime. But that was not to last. The politically desperate Tamil leadership was soon back to its old ways and put its faith in the UNP. Meanwhile, the militants had become more aggressive and in the name of Tamil solidarity threatened left candidates against contesting the DDC elections and forced the Nava Samasamaja Party (NSSP) to withdraw its nominations.

Jayawardane won in the presidential election of October 1982, which his popular opponent Sirimavo Bandaranaike (widow of SWRD Bandaranaike, and Prime Minister, 1960-65 and 1970-77) could not contest since he had in 1980 stripped her of her civic rights. Then he proceeded to deliver a body blow to parliamentary democracy by extended the life of the parliament by a further six years by conducting a referendum in December 1982. In both the presidential election and the referendum the Tamils of the North and the East demonstrated their displeasure with Jayawardane, who returned the compliment by intensifying brutality by the armed forces in the North, leading to an escalation of armed conflict between the armed forces and the youth and the holocaust of 1983.

By 1983, the TULF was so badly isolated from the masses in the North that most Tamil MPs avoided visiting their electorates, initially for fear of embarrassment and later fear for their own lives. When the pogrom of 1983 was unleashed following the killing of 13 Sinhalese soldiers in an LTTE ambush, no part of the country was safe for Tamils. While government-backed mobs attacked Tamils in the South, the armed forces went on the rampage in the North and East. Unlike in 1958 and 1977, the Tamils had nowhere to go. The TULF had no answers, nor did the Tamil militants at the time. While the TULF leaders fled the country to save their lives, the militants stayed on; and the militants who crossed the waters of the Palk Straits had other things in mind as did the host government of India.

The holocaust had effectively destroyed the credibility of the moderate political leadership, although a few retained credibility on an individual basis, but not as leaders.

Less Spoken Aspects of Tamil Politics. A monolithic image of Tamil politics had come into being since the FP came to the fore in 1956. This was accompanied by a tendency to underplay the significance of caste and class oppression in the name of the struggle for Tamil rights. The discussion of caste and class, even today, is denounced by some as an attempt to divide the Tamils, even with the Tamil nationalists bitterly divided among themselves on politically less important issues.

To understand the conduct of the Tamil nationalist leadership during the past century, it is important to recognise its class loyalties. The fact that P Kandiah, of the CP, was the only leftist to be elected from the North demonstrates the power of conservative thought in the North. Tamil nationalist political parties were dominated by the elite of the Vellala caste: but for the election a member of a depressed caste to the Senate in 1957 by the FP with backing of LSSP MPs, until 1977, neither the ACTC nor the FP fielded a candidate from the depressed castes comprising 30% of the population of the Jaffna peninsula. A candidate from among them was fielded in 1977. But that was after the successful mass movement against caste oppression led by the Marxist Leninists in 1966-71, the defeat of Messrs Amirthalingam and Sivasithamparam at the polls in 1970 by the increasingly assertive depressed castes, and the creation of the electorate of Udupiddy with a sizeable depressed caste community.

The FP consistently portrayed the left, especially the communists who were a stronger political force than the LSSP in the North, as traitors to the Tamil cause. Such labelling was possible since the left lent support to the SLFP, which it saw as more progressive than the unashamedly pro-imperialist UNP. While the FP drew attention to the Sinhala chauvinism of the SLFP, it took no notice of the anti-imperialist and other progressive aspects of the SLFP. This approach was necessary, since highlighting issues of social justice will invariably concede a greater role for the left among Tamils. Thus the FP remained a single-issue party, which saw the language problem as the main problem facing the Tamils.

The betrayal of the working class and with it the minorities by the parliamentary left by entering into a coalition with the SLFP (the LSSP since 1964 and the CP since 1970) made it possible for the FP leadership to insincerely brand the entire left as traitors, although it knew that that a sizeable section of the left had split from the opportunists and as ever stood for the rights of the Tamils. But what is often forgotten is that the old left, which led the working class and the masses in the General Strike of July 1947 and the 1953 *Hartal*, had let down the working class in the interest of electoral politics well before it let down the Tamils. The peak point of the treachery of the old left was its betrayal of a united struggle by the workers based on 21 demands, which included political demands and addressed problems faced by the entire working class of the country. The demands, to which the trade unions affiliated to the three main left parties were signatories, had overwhelming support from the working class across the country. But the trade union action planned in 1963 was aborted by the MEP and the LSSP being tempted in turn, and the latter successfully, by the prospect of joining the SLFP government, which feared a strike based on political demands besides economic ones.

The ACTC and the FP under various pretexts opposed the SLFP-led government moves between 1956 and 1959 such as asking the British to leave their naval and air bases in the country, nationalising the Colombo Harbour under the control of foreign companies, nationalising the private bus monopolies to make bus services more accessible to the rural population, and even the half-hearted Paddy Lands Bill designed to curtail exploitation by big landowners. This pattern was repeated when the SLFP government (1960-65) nationalised foreign oil trading companies, with the leader of the FP denouncing the step as unrighteous. The FP sided with the Christian and Catholic missionaries when in 1960 the government took over state assisted-schools, where the state paid the bills and the missionaries ran the schools. Notably, the state allowed the option for the schools to go private, but prohibited charging a mandatory fee from the children; and some of the leading schools took the option. Here the ACTC and the FP actually defended the Tamil elitist interest, since the Hindu schools in Jaffna and to a less extent Protestant Christian schools were bastions of Vellala elitism. Discriminatory practices denied the 'untouchables' access to education beyond primary school, and sometimes even to primary education. Nationalisation placed the management of schools in the public domain and, in fact, boosted the educational aspirations of the socially backward.

Tamil nationalist hostility towards the local communists was extended to the Soviet Union and China. (Notably, it was the SLFP-led government of 1956-60 that established diplomatic relations with the socialist countries). In the border conflict between China and India in 1961, the FP was even more vehement than the UNP in denouncing China as the aggressor, without examining the facts. Also, soon after the April 1971 insurrection by the JVP was subdued, the FP joined the UNP to falsely accuse China of supporting the JVP. Hostility towards

China has persisted among the Tamil nationalists, many of whom still portray China (but not the US or Israel) as a friend of the Sinhala chauvinist state, and a threat to Indian interests.

The Anti-Left Trend in Tamil Nationalism. The anti-left mindset of the FP relates to its class nature. Although the FP started as a populist alternative to the conservative ACTC, which it overcame in 1956, it inherited the mantle of the ACTC to serve the same Tamil elite class interests. Understandably, the FP saw the Vietnam liberation struggle in the 1960s as communist trouble-making and denounced the struggle against caste oppression in the North as a communist effort to make a Vietnam out of Jaffna.

Another line of thinking that has haunted Tamil nationalist thinking since around the time of the failed Satyagraha of 1961 and persists even after turning to armed struggle against an oppressor backed by imperialism is the desire to emulate Israel. Some Tamil nationalists imagined parallels between the Tamils and Jews and drew inspiration from the Zionist forefathers of Israel. After 1977, however, a section of the youth realised that valid parallels were with the Palestinians, and some Tamil militant groups even received combat training from the PLO from the late 1970s until the early 1980s, when the Indian establishment began to play godfather.

With the fading of the British Empire, the FP saw in the US its salvation, especially when the SLFP was in power, since the SLFP was in American eyes too close to the 'reds'. Despite a strong feeling of kinship with India because of a shared cultural heritage and common language with Tamilnadu, there were reservations about India's role since the Nehru clan was warm towards the Bandaranaikes, although the former resented Sri Lankan neutrality in the Sino-Indian border dispute and Sri Lanka allowing Pakistani military aircraft to refuel in Colombo during the war preceding the formation of Bangladesh.

Although the FP at the time of its founding called itself socialist, with the exception of the *Hartal* of 1953, it never sided with the working classes against capitalism or imperialism. Another manifestation of this approach was that the FP consciously distanced itself from any form of struggle in the

South for social justice, explaining its aloofness in terms of its limiting its interests to the Tamil cause. Thus it was no accident that R Sampanthan, later to become an important leader of the TULF, in his maiden speech in parliament in 1978 spoke approvingly of the policy of economic liberalisation announced by the UNP government. Sadly, this reactionary streak in Tamil nationalism has survived a quarter century of armed struggle against Sinhala chauvinism backed by US imperialism.

Other Significant Events and Trends. The economy of the Jaffna Peninsula, home to the majority of the Tamils, depended considerably on earnings from small trade and wages earned outside the peninsula, so much so that it used to be light-heartedly referred to as a 'money-order economy'. Employment in the police and the armed forces was relatively low. Systematic discrimination in state employment and education meant that Tamil presence in state jobs declined to levels far below the percentage population. Tamil recruitment to the armed forces became negligible since the 1960s and that to the police declined to levels so low that by the 1970s in several police stations in the East it became very difficult to deal with the police in Tamil; this pattern became true of the North from the 1980s.

There was no significant state investment in industry in the North and East since the 1950s, in contrast to the large number of medium and large industries established in the South with state funding and foreign 'aid', and instances of investment in the East were such that they encouraged Sinhala settlement. Even after the UNP government declared its open economic policy in 1978, investment in the North and East was discouraged by the state, except where it fell in line with its chauvinist programme.

Economic tragedy in the North was averted by two developments in the 1970s. The government was compelled by balance of payments problems, partly due to the 'Oil Crisis' of the early 1970s, to restrict the import of non-essential goods and several items of agricultural produce such as chillies, potatoes and onions which could be grown locally. This boosted agricultural production in the Jaffna peninsula, where for the first time the agricultural small producers experienced a sense of well being. This also contributed to a thirst for land, and many people from the peninsula began to venture out to put to use land lying to the south of the peninsula. Thus, the Tamil population became politically aware of the question of land as a result of economic reality rather than Tamil national awareness.

By this time the government was determined to contain Tamil settlements and the issue had become increasingly political. While Tamil settlers faced risks and threats on an increasing scale, illegal settlement of Sinhalese, often in strategically chosen locations with the backing of the armed forces and for clearly chauvinistic political reasons, proceeded unhindered alongside a growth in Sinhala population induced by expanding economic activity. Demographic changes in the East gained impetus in the 1980s under the Mahaweli Project, the largest single irrigation and hydropower scheme to be undertaken in the country, which was implemented in a way that Tamils were effectively excluded.

The second development also related to the 'Oil Crisis', and concerned employment in the Middle East. Tamils sought and secured employment in various service sectors and in the professions in the Middle East as well as in the growing economies of Africa. This was to be a mixed blessing: while on the one hand it provided badly needed economic relief, it had an adverse impact on the tradition of frugality and hard work in the North and, in the context of worsening relationship between the nationalities and distrust in the government, on the attitude of the middle class youth in what was essentially a conservative society.

With Tamil nationalism as the main resistance to the Sinhala chauvinist agenda, it was inevitable that the chauvinists transformed the Sinhala-Tamil contradiction into a hostile contradiction. However, until 1977, the government interfered, although not always with an adequate sense of responsibility, to ensure that the conflict did not escalate into ethnic war. The attitude of the UNP government elected in 1977 was different, and from the outset was provocatively confrontational.

Chauvinist Challenge to Other Nationalities. Although the Tamils had been the main target of Sinhala chauvinism since

1948, the Hill Country Tamils continued to be targeted 'lawfully' under the Sirima-Shastri Pact of 1964 and by the closing down of tea estates following nationalisation in 1974, and unlawfully by chauvinistic acts of violence including arson, forced expulsion from the estates and other misdeeds. The Hill Country Tamils have at times succeeded in resisting chauvinist aggression, but remain vulnerable to state sponsored moves to displace them: under the Mahaweli scheme in the early 1980s and more recently the Upper Kotmale Hydropower scheme and the resettlement of Sinhalese victims of natural disasters. Attacks against the Hill Country Tamils have escalated since the nationalisation of the tea estates and, since the escalation of the conflict in the North East, the linguistic affinity between the Tamils and the Hill Country Tamils is used by the security forces to harass and persecute Hill Country Tamils in the name of combating Tamil terrorism. Chauvinistic harassment and the failure of the Hill Country Tamil leadership to stand up for its people has driven some Hill Country Tamil youth towards the LTTE, but not in significant numbers.

The Muslims in the East suffered as a result of acquisition of land by the state, colonisation and illegal settlements. In the West, there have, from time to time, been major acts of violence directed against the Muslim community starting with the police firing on Muslims in a mosque in Puttalam in 1976 up to the attack on Muslims in Dharga Town in 2006. Muslim businesses have been systematically targeted by organisations close to the chauvinistic Sihala Urumaya, now Jathika Hela Urumaya (JHU). Sinhala chauvinist resentment of Muslims gathered new momentum following the often dubious benefit to the Muslims from employment in the Middle East, new trade opportunities, and aid from certain Arab countries.

The grievances of the Muslims and the demand of the Muslims for an autonomous region in the East are encouraged by a section of the chauvinists merely to weaken the Tamil demand for autonomy and to widen the rift between Tamil and Muslim communities. However, no opportunity is spared to make inroads into Muslim controlled businesses and territories. It should also be noted that a section of the Sinhala Buddhist elite has over the past two decades solicited the support of a section of the Tamil Hindu elite with affinity to the Vishwa Hindu Parishad and the Indian saffron brigade to promote anti-Muslim and anti-Christian sentiments.

Class and Chauvinistic Politics. It is true that the petit bourgeois classes have been the main base for chauvinist electoral politics. The class interests served by the main chauvinist parties have, however, been those of the feudal-capitalist classes; and it was the rivalry between sections of this elite and their relationship to foreign capital that once marked the difference between the UNP and the SLFP and the nature of the alliances formed by them. The reactionary feudal-capitalist classes have continued to cynically manipulate nationalist sentiments to divide the people along ethnic lines, and have been encouraged by imperialism to do so. Significantly, chauvinists and narrow nationalists who express strong sentiments about preserving traditional social values turn a blind eye to the adverse effects of imperialist globalisation on various aspects of social life.

The old left through its opportunist alliance with the SLFP, initially for electoral advantage and subsequently for a share in state power, compromised its working class loyalty; and its corruption infected the affiliated trade unions. The rise of chauvinism also helped to divide the trade unions, especially the white collar unions, on ethnic lines. The political degeneration of left-dominated trade unions made it possible not only for the SLFP but also the UNP to make inroads into the trade union movement. Following the erosion of the electoral base of the old left, the JVP made its entry into white-collar trade unions and used a mix of chauvinist ideology and left slogans to expand its base. Thus the weakening of working class politics along with the subjugation of working class interests to electoral politics has contributed in no small measure to the rise of chauvinism.

4

The National Question as War

The anti-Tamil pogrom of July 1983 marked the escalation of a conflict between the state and Tamil nationalists into a war against the Tamil nationality. There is reason to believe that this escalation of the national conflict was a well calculated strategy by the government to divert the attention of the Sinhala masses from economic issues, and in particular its plans to liberalise the economy, privatise state-controlled ventures and 'reform' social services in line with the dictates of the IMF, the World Bank, and the Asian Development Bank. Despite a steamroller majority for the government to pass any legislation at will and an executive presidency with virtually unlimited power, privatisation of services, especially education (provided free by the state from primary school to university) and health services (provided free in government hospitals), and the removal of food and other subsidies would have met with strong public resistance. In fact, no previous government, including the UNP, dared to attack these institutions or to privatise any venture that had been nationalised.

Some argue that the change in economic conditions caused by the open economic policy led to the sharpening of the ethnic conflict. This argument seeks to deflect the blame for the transformation of the ethnic conflict into war away from the historic role of chauvinistic politics with successive governments pandering to chauvinism. It also inverts the sequence of events, since it was the escalation of the national contradiction that enabled the government to pass legislation that could be used to put down any form of popular resistance, and to beef up the armed forces. Not surprisingly, neither the repressive legislation nor the militarization of the state has been a matter of concern to imperialism.

Although the scale of the anti-Tamil violence of 1983 sent shock waves across the world because of unexpected media publicity, the imperialist countries (or the international community as they like to be called) did not bring pressure on the Sri Lankan government to resolve the national question or to protect the rights of all its citizens. While Sri Lanka was ritually warned at various international fora against its violation of human and fundamental rights, the imperialists kept up their economic backing as well as military and strategic support for the government.

Build-up to the Showdown of 1987. Taking advantage of the climate of fear following the violence of 1983, the government diverted attention from its role in planning and executing the pogrom by proscribing the JVP, the NSSP and the CP, and passed the Sixth Amendment to the Constitution making espousal, promotion, financing, encouraging or advocacy of the establishment of a separate state in Sri Lanka illegal, thus making it necessary for the TULF MPs to formally abandon their demand for Tamil Eelam to continue to sit in parliament. Meantime, the Indian government on the one hand applied pressure on the Sri Lankan government to end the ethnic conflict and on the other wanted a major role for India in that matter. It should be noted that a considerable number of Tamil militants were already receiving combat training in India, with the knowledge if not encouragement of its government, and the number shot up after July 1983.

On the political front, talks initiated in December 1983 between the two countries led to an All-Party Conference on devolution of powers in January 1984 but the Sri Lankan government abandoned the proposals of the conference. The assassination of Indira Gandhi in 1984 October led to an apparent change in India's approach to the Sri Lankan national question, but it is doubtful if the aims of the Indian establishment were altered by the event. The Indian establishment, besides taking the TULF under its wing, also patronised the five main Tamil liberation militant organisations (EROS, EPRLF, LTTE, PLOTE, and TELO) and a number of smaller organisations through its various agencies including the notorious Research and Analysis Wing (RAW); and guided their political, and to some extent military, strategy. Following the failure of the talks between Sri Lankan Tamil parties and the Sri Lankan government, held in Thimpu, Bhutan under Indian patronage, another Sri Lanka All-Party Conference was convened in June 1985 to resolve the national question but got nowhere. The rival Tamil militants, while being covert beneficiaries of the largesse of the Indian establishment, also cultivated their Tamilnadu political patrons out of mutual interest. By 1987, all but the LTTE and a few minor organisations which for ideological reasons rejected Indian patronage, had surrendered their independence to their Indian patrons.

On the battlefront, Tamil militant activity escalated, with bomb explosions at the Meenambakkam Airport in Tamilnadu, India (August 1984), various locations in Colombo (October 1984), and in an Air Lanka aircraft at the Katunayake Airport (1986 May), and the shameful gunning down of 250 Sinhalese civilians in Anuradhapura (May 1985) with alleged logistic support from Indian undercover agents. While the government armed forces continued to harass Tamils in the North and the East, militants continued with political assassinations, setting new precedents like the killing of two former TULF MPs in 1985, so that the targets were no more restricted to 'Tamil traitors' or the 'enemy'. Leading members and cadres of rival movements as well as dissenters in leading militant organisations suffered brutal treatment. Indian patrons of the militants turned a blind eye to such events, and had been directly or indirectly responsible for several of the problems.

Organised violence targeting civilians escalated from 1984. In 1985 June, Sinhala chauvinists supported by the armed forces ruthlessly attacked Tamil villages in the Trincomalee District killing over 150 within two weeks; several hundred Tamil villages were destroyed and hundreds of Tamil civilians were killed in the months that followed. Tamil militants, in turn, killed Sinhalese civilians in large numbers. In April 1987, 128 Sinhalese bus passengers were brutally massacred and another 50 injured on the Habarana-Trincomalee road. This was soon followed by a bomb explosion killing 113 persons and injuring more than 300 in Pettah, Colombo. Shortly afterwards, the government launched a massive military operation called 'Operation Liberation' at Vadamaratchi (the north eastern part of the Jaffna peninsula) to put an end to the dominance of the LTTE in Jaffna, which was already facing a blockade denying transport of goods to the peninsula.

The IPKF Misadventure. The subsequent turn of events was rapid, with the showdown between the governments of India and Sri Lanka over sending essential supplies to the North culminating in the signing of the Indo-Lanka Peace Accord on 27th July 1987. The Indian government had obtained under duress the consent of the LTTE leader to abide by the accord and to disarm the LTTE, and lost no time to land the Indian Peace Keeping Force (IPKF) on Sri Lankan soil starting 30th July 1987.

While most of the Tamils welcomed the accord, the Sinhalese had mixed feelings, based on the aspects concerning the national question. But there was more to the accord than that, and the less spoken parts of the Accord explicitly placed restrictions on Sri Lankan foreign and defence policy, asserting India's position as the regional hegemon. The vast majority of the left and progressive forces in the South welcomed the Accord. Only the Left Communist Party, since renamed the New Democratic Party (NDP), made a comprehensive criticism of the Accord and warned that it would not lead to the resolution of the national question but pave the way for Indian hegemony. Concerns about implications for the sovereignty of the country were expressed by Sirima Bandaranaike, the leader of the SLFP, whose civic rights had only been restored a year earlier by JR Jayawardane; but the main objection of the SLFP was to the setting up of provincial governments with a merged North-East province. There was dissent within the ranks of the UNP as well; but it was the chauvinistic JVP that was to make political capital of popular concerns.

Following the 13th amendment to the constitution in November 1987 that made provisions for the setting up of Provincial Councils, a bitter campaign was launched by the JVP, initially with the support of the SLFP, which was soon sidelined by the JVP. The campaign escalated into an insurrection accompanied by a hate campaign against everything Indian. The JVP used terror tactics to stall the functioning of the government; and R Premadasa, a UNP leader who opposed the Accord, was elected president in 1998 December, with covert support from the JVP. The JVP insurrection continued unabated and Premadasa used the anti-terrorism laws designed to put down Tamil separatists to combat the JVP. By late 1989, when the JVP's campaign of destruction and terror was finally overcome by state terror, which annihilated all but one member of the politburo of the JVP, well over 60,000 persons, mostly Sinhala youth, had been killed or abducted and presumed killed, mainly by the government forces. JVP killings included an estimated 6000 left and democratic political activists, including Vijaya Kumaranatunga (the husband of former President Chandrika Kumaratunga) who was a popular figure supporting the Accord, as well as several important UNP personalities. The leader of the NSSP, Vickramabahu Karunaratna was shot and critically wounded by a JVP attacker but saved by surgical intervention. It should be noted here that, in the North, leaders of NDP and the NSSP were issued death threats by Tamil militants, the LTTE in particular, following an effective campaign in support of Sirima Bandaranaike against Premadasa in the 1998 presidential election. The NDP leaders successfully evaded their potential assassins, but Annamalai, the leader of the Jaffna branch of the NSSP, was killed as were several left sympathisers.

The LTTE was deeply suspicious of the Accord and Indian intentions, and was easily provoked by the clumsy handling of a delicate situation by the Indian High Commission and the IPKF. With the government armed forces in the South preoccupied with the JVP insurrection and the forces in the North and East confined to barracks, armed conflict erupted between the LTTE and the IPKF. The latter proved vulnerable to the guerrilla tactics of the LTTE; and the heavy-handed response of the IPKF and incidents of misconduct by IPKF personnel further antagonised the people. The net result was that the people of Jaffna suffered a severe loss of life and property and the IPKF lost many soldiers.

The Eelam People's Revolutionary Liberation Front (EPRLF), a client of the Indian establishment, was elected to power in the North-East Provincial Government in October 1988 under dubious circumstances, and acted in ways that alienated it from the people. Eventually, abandoned by a defeated IPKF, opposed by a contemptuous Sri Lankan government, and cornered by a hostile LTTE, the EPRLF leadership made its last desperate bid for survival by unilaterally declaring the independence of Tamil Eelam in 1990, and fled the country in ignominy.

President Premadasa, known for his resentment of the Accord and the presence of the IPKF, backed the LTTE in its campaign against the IPKF and called for its withdrawal. With the JVP defeated in the South and the IPKF on the retreat in the North East, Premadasa demanded the withdrawal of the IPKF by the end of the 1989; the IPKF withdrew early next year, following the change of government in India. He took advantage of the unilateral declaration of the independence by the EPRLF to dismiss the Provincial Government of the North-East and take direct control of the North-East.

The LTTE Takes Over. Undeniably, the Indo-Sri Lanka Peace Accord was the first comprehensive accord concerning the national question that any Sri Lankan government went some way towards implementing. However, the Accord itself was seriously flawed and addressed the national question merely as a Sinhala-Tamil issue and sought to assert Indian regional hegemonic interests. In drafting it, there was no consultation with the Tamils, especially the main Tamil militant force, the LTTE. In its implementation, the IPKF and the Indian High Commission showed little understanding of the underlying issues. Nor were they equipped to deal with the consequences of the Accord in a way that would help the resolution of the problem. Thus Sri Lanka was left with a worse problem than before the Accord.

As the IPKF retreated and finally withdrew, the LTTE moved in to take absolute control of much of the North and East. In 1990 February, for the first time, a Sri Lankan government held formal talks with Tamil militants. Although the relationship between the government and the LTTE was superficially warm, there was mutual distrust as well as the intention to undermine each other. This soon led to the second phase of war at a great cost to the lives and livelihood of the people in the North-East and to the country's economy.

The LTTE made its biggest political blunder in antagonising the Muslims, firstly by mass killings in the East and then by expelling Muslims wholesale from the North. The erroneous approach towards the Muslims arose from a refusal to recognise a separate identity for them and the demand that the Muslims gave unqualified support to the Tamil militants in the same way that the Tamils had been conditioned to.

The killing of the leaders of the EPRLF (Pathmanabha faction) in Chennai and TULF leaders Amirthalingam and Yogeswaran in Colombo confirmed that the LTTE, like other leading Tamil militant movements, placed the gun in command. The assassination of Rajeev Gandhi in 1991, denied to this day by the LTTE, dealt a severe blow to the LTTE support base in Tamilnadu, from which it has not quite recovered. It also made it politically expedient for the corrupt and opportunist DMK and ADMK dominating Tamilnadu politics to distance themselves from the LTTE as well as from the demand for a separate Tamil Eelam.

From Talks for Peace to War for Peace. Dissent grew within the UNP government, and in 1991 an elitist faction moved unsuccessfully to impeach the President Premadasa for his undemocratic conduct of state affairs. The UNP dissidents left the party to form the Democratic United National Front in August 1991. Its leader Lalith Athulathmudali was shot dead, later alleged to be by forces loyal to Premadasa, during an election campaign meeting in April 1993 for the Western Provincial Council. This was followed soon after by the assassination of Premadasa on May Day 1993 and of the UNP presidential candidate Gamini Dissanayake the following year. Chandrika Kumaratunga, who returned to the fold of the SLFP in 1992 after splitting from it in the mid-80s to join the Sri Lanka Mahajana Pakshayaya (SLMP) founded by her husband Vijaya Kumaranatunga (killed by the JVP in 1989). She promised an end to war and a peaceful resolution of the national question, and was elected President with a 60% mandate by a war weary people.

The first few months of the Kumaratunga presidency raised hopes; but the sloppy handling of the negotiations with the LTTE led to an end to the unilateral ceasefire declared by the LTTE in 1994 following her election. Fierce battles followed, and in October 1995 the government drove the LTTE out of its stronghold in Jaffna, a virtual centre of parallel government. Under pressure from the LTTE, the people fled Jaffna to LTTE held areas, but most of them returned as the situation stabilised.

The turn of events led to reconciliation between the LTTE and the TULF. The LTTE, having learnt from its tactical blunder in calling for a Tamil boycott of the elections in 1994 which let the Eelam People's Democratic Front (which splintered from the EPRLF) secure a large number of seats in parliament with a handful of votes and thereby an important ministry which it used to build a base for itself in the North, decided to support, first indirectly and later more openly, a group dominated by the TULF (and named the Tamil National Alliance in 2001) in the elections that followed. The Tamil leaders who owed their parliamentary seats to the LTTE acted in consultation with it and endorsed the LTTE's claim to be the sole representative of the Tamils in peace negotiations. Thus, the TNA (now called the FP, because of complications caused by a split in the TNA), despite its inherent loyalty to the Indian establishment, was shunned by the latter favouring Tamil politicians hostile to the LTTE, even when they had been rejected by the Tamils at the elections.

In 1996 President Kumaratunga submitted by to the Parliamentary Select Committee a devolution package aimed at addressing through legislation some of the main grievances of the Tamils. The package, owing to Sinhala chauvinist pressure from within the ruling alliance and without, was already a severely watered version of what was conceived in 1994, and failed to please the Tamil leadership. In August 2000 she presented in Parliament a bill to enable devolution of power, which was withdrawn following unruly conduct by the UNP and other chauvinistic opponents to the bill.

An ill-advised attack on the historic Temple of the Tooth in Kandy in 1998 by the LTTE led to a ban on the LTTE and a set-back for campaigners for peace. Escalation of the war by the government led to unprecedented loss of life, displacement of people and loss of home, property and livelihood. The initial territorial gains by the government were soon reversed and subsequently the government lost more territory than it gained, including a major army camp in Mullaitivu and the strategically important Elephant Pass.

An attempt on the life of Kumaratunga, allegedly by the LTTE, on the eve of the presidential election in December 1999, helped her re-election. However, subsequent LTTE attacks on selected economic targets in the South hurt the economy and the popularity of the government, and forced Kumaratunga to seek the services of Norway, whose assistance she had used for monitoring ceasefire as early as 1995, to facilitate peace negotiations; but progress was slow owing to severe pressure from the chauvinists. At the end of April 2000, the LTTE nearly overran the main army camp in Jaffna, but signals from India that it may intervene on the humanitarian pretext of saving the lives of Sri Lankan soldiers appear to have deterred the LTTE from fighting to a finish. Humiliating defeats of the government military campaigns up to 2001, termed the Orwellian-sounding 'War for Peace', led to the strengthening of the LTTE both militarily and politically.

Renewed Hopes for Peace. The destruction of half the fleet of SriLankan Airlines by suicide bombers in 2001 made a big impact, while political horse-trading by the UNP later in the year led to fresh elections and to a UNP-led United National Front (UNF) coalition government in December 2001. The LTTE unilaterally declared a ceasefire which was soon followed by a ceasefire agreement (CFA) and a memorandum of understanding (MoU) between the government and the LTTE in 2002. Peace negotiations started in Thailand in September 2002 were followed by a second round in November, also in Thailand, and a third in Norway in December, where the LTTE indicated willingness to consider a federal solution in place of its call for a separate state. Progress was poor in subsequent rounds (Thailand, January 2003, Germany, February 2003 and Japan, March 2003) owing to obstacles placed by the armed forces and the failure of the government to deliver on what had been agreed in the earlier meetings on matters including the resettlement of the displaced and rebuilding the war affected Tamil areas.

The process started to stall after the talks in Germany and ground to a halt after the meeting in Japan. The LTTE opted out of the talks indefinitely, and rejected three successive proposals by the government for the resumption of talks on the grounds that they were inadequate to deal with the issues concerned, and put forward in June 2003 a comprehensive proposal for an interim self-governing authority (ISGA) for the North-East as a step towards solving the national question.

End of the Road for Peace Talks. President Kumaratunga took advantage of the impasse in which the UNF government found itself following the LTTE proposal and used her executive powers to bring crucial ministries directly under her to render ineffective the peace process. She dismissed the politically weakened UNF government, dissolved parliament, and the PA and the JVP formed an opportunistic alliance, the Sandanaya, which was elected to power in April 2004 at a price to the PA, and bigger one to the prospects for peace.

Despite the lack of progress in solving the national question and the failure to restore normal life in war affected regions, the cessation of hostilities between the armed forces and the LTTE gave the people of the North-East a badly needed respite, which lasted nearly four years since the unilateral declaration of ceasefire by the LTTE in 2001. But moves behind the scenes to undermine the CFA involved a range of subversive activities like the attack on a Chinese vessel some distance outside what the LTTE claimed to be its territorial waters and inciting clashes between Tamils and Muslims with the connivance of certain Muslim political leaders. Even more cynically, a split was engineered in the ranks of the LTTE by US undercover agents, on the request of the leader of the UNP, while peace talks were in progress, as revealed at the time of the presidential election in 2005. The split that occurred in March 2004 was led by Karuna (V Muralitharan), the leader of the Eastern Command of the LTTE who was a participant in the peace talks. Karuna's group, called the Tamil Makkal Viduthalai Pulikal (TMVP), was militarily defeated by the LTTE, but survived with the help of the government armed forces and made life difficult for the LTTE by killing leaders and members of the LTTE in the East, as well as Tamil politicians sympathetic to the LTTE.

The prospects for peace received another blow with the tsunami of 26th December 2004. The North-East and the South were badly hit and Mullaitivu in the north east of the island where the LTTE naval base is located was one of the worst hit areas. The partiality of the government in distributing international relief to the refugees and, besides deliberate neglect, obstruction by the armed forces of the transport of essential supplies to affected areas under LTTE control was a bad sign. Partly under international pressure, President Kumaratunga agreed to set up the P-TOMS (Post-Tsunami Operational Management Structure) by which the government and LTTE would cooperate to provide essential relief to tsunami victims in LTTE-controlled areas. The P-TOMS was abandoned when the JVP, which initiated a mass campaign against it, secured a court ruling based on legal technicalities against its implementation.

Towards an Undeclared War. Meantime, chauvinists opposed to the peace process saw in the split in the LTTE and the impact of the tsunami on the economy in LTTE controlled areas and on the military capability of the LTTE, an opportunity to annihilate the LTTE. Such thinking had its adherents in high places in the armed forces and in the ruling coalition. Escalation of the conflict thus seemed inevitable.

The election of Mahinda Rajapaksha in November 2005 was

made possible by a last-minute call by LTTE for a boycott of the presidential election. Notably, a politically more meaningful call by the NDP several weeks before the election, asking the people of the North-East to spoil their ballot papers, was not even considered by the LTTE; and it was alleged in early 2007 that the LTTE was bribed by a member of the Rajapaksha clan to call for the boycott. While the charge against the LTTE is serious and if true a betrayal of the trust of the Tamil people, it is doubtful whether the prospects for peace would have been brighter if the UNP candidate was elected president.

Proscription of the LTTE by Canada in April 2006 and by the EU in May 2006 under pressure from the US applied through the UK did not help the peace process. The LTTE was already proscribed by India in 1991, following information linking it to the assassination of Rajeev Gandhi, by the US in 1997 and by the UK 2001. Although the Kumaratunga government claimed credit for the ban by the US and UK, let there be no doubt that the measures against the LTTE were taken in the self-interest of the governments concerned, and not to please the Sri Lankan government. The ban by the EU, rather than make the LTTE more flexible in its approach as claimed by the advocates of the ban, hardened its attitude, while the Sri Lankan government saw in it a licence to destroy at will. The EU ban also hurt the performance of the ceasefire monitoring mission set-up under the CFA, which from then on was observed only in breach.

From the outset President Rajapaksha showed little interest in peace talks with the LTTE, and used objections from his chauvinistic allies, the JVP and the JHU, as pretexts to hamper a peaceful resolution of the conflict. Talks were arranged in 2006 by the Norwegian intermediaries with great difficulty, the first in Geneva and the next in Oslo. The escalation of violence, violation of the CFA and support for the TMVP paramilitaries from the armed forces of the government to attack the LTTE became the central issues. The talks came to naught because the government failed to honour agreements reached in the Geneva round on the question of the paramilitaries. The Oslo round was doomed to fail even before it started because of endless disputes that preceded it on matters like transport, which only a year earlier would have been minor issues.

War Undeclared and Declared. An attempt on the life of the Army Commander Sarath Fonseka in April 2006 served as the pretext for a series of bombing raids; and the dispute over a waterway in the East led to an escalation of the conflict. The LTTE has been held responsible for anti-personnel mine attacks on the armed forces, the use of suicide bombers against senior officers of the armed forces and politicians, killing leading political opponents, and fatal attacks on innocent Sinhala civilians who had little to do with the conflict. Killings, kidnappings and threats had become part of everyday life in the North-East and the targets were not just members and supporters of LTTE or those hostile to LTTE, but also other civilians. The government forces have used every alleged LTTE attack as pretext for retaliation. Civilians in the locality have been attacked following minor skirmishes with the LTTE, and whole communities on other occasions. Since mid-2006 people living in LTTE-controlled areas in the East were driven out by indiscriminate bombing raids by Israeli-built K'fir aircraft and MIG fighters, and artillery and multi-barrel rocket launcher (MBRL) attacks against civilian targets, which were claimed to be strategic LTTE targets.

The ceasefire had become a shambles by 2006 and the political climate ensured that attempts to revive it and restart peace talks would fail. The government formally withdrew from the CFA in February 2008, only to formalise a war that had been in full swing since 2006. Nearly three years of the Rajapaksha presidency has steered the country from uncertain peace through an undeclared war to declared war, and unprecedented mass destruction in the North-East. This has been accompanied by a political climate marked by an unending spate of acts of extortion, kidnapping, 'disappearing', death threats and murder, much of it in broad daylight not only in the troubled North-East but also in Colombo. Neutral observers have often indicted the armed forces and the police as accomplices. The victims are predominantly but not exclusively Tamils. There is evidence that Sinhalese who are openly critical of the war have especially been targeted.

From the middle of 2006, the Batticaloa district in the East had became a massive refuge camp. In March-April 2007 the number of internally displaced persons in the North East swelled by 200,000 or more, owing to intense bombing and shelling by the Sri Lankan armed forces, which finally drove the LTTE from its strongholds in the East. In the wake of the military success in the East, the government sought to extend the war to the North. Heavy bombing and intense artillery attack have helped the armed forces to capture the western half of LTTE-held territory in the North, and displaced an estimated 300,000 or more people. The tendency for the vast majority of the war-displaced in the North to drift towards LTTE-held rather than government-held territory is an expression of distrust in the government.

The LTTE seems to have made a strategic retreat from the East without many casualties, and its cadres remaining in the East seem to have regrouped to launch guerrilla attacks in recent months on a modest scale against the armed forces and the TMVP in the Amparai and Batticaloa Districts as well as in adjoining areas. While the LTTE is by no means poised to score a military victory, it has repeatedly shown its capability for surprise attacks by ramming an explosive laden truck into a naval convoy and launching an attack by sea on the Galle Harbour in October 2006 and by its air strikes using light aircraft starting with the one on the Air Force base at Katunayake in March 2007. The air attacks in recent months especially have called into question the defence capability of the armed forces. Thus, given the stiff resistance put up by the LTTE on the northern battle front, the government aim to make a clean sweep of the LTTE controlled territory is unlikely to be fulfilled soon.

The government took advantage of its military success in the East to hastily resettle the majority of the war-displaced persons without restoring the necessary infrastructure and to conduct elections to local authorities in the Batticaloa District followed by elections to the de-merged Eastern Provincial Council. The elections were by no means free or fair. The UNP and the SLMC boycotted the local elections, but contested the Provincial Council elections. Soon after making Pillayan (Sivanesathurai Chandrakanthan), who replaced Karuna as the effective leader of the TMVP, the Chief Minister of the powerless Eastern Provincial Council, the government inducted Karuna as MP as a check against Pillayan. The result has been a sharp rise in violent crimes including abduction and murder in the Batticaloa district, giving the lie to government claims that normalcy has returned to the East.

Another worrying development since early 2007 is that attacks on media personnel and political personalities have been extended to the Sinhala community as well. This is seen as a concerted effort to silence by a variety of means all political opposition to the Sinhala chauvinist agenda and to a newly emergent junta. The killing of Janaka Perera, former army commander and leading UNP candidate in the recent elections to the North Central Provincial Council, was blamed on the LTTE by the government, but the UNP and other critics have suggested government responsibility by pointing to the denial of personal security to Janaka Perera and the disrespect shown to him following his killing

Expulsion of local and international non-government organisations (NGOs and INGOs) from the North-East since 2007 culminated in the withdrawal of the United Nations agencies from the LTTE-controlled parts of the North in September 2008 leaving the ICRC as the only international humanitarian organization with a permanent presence there. The expulsions have on the one hand aggravated the humanitarian crisis in the North-East and on the other restricted access to information on the deteriorating humanitarian situation in the region.

The country is in an impasse on the national question, and the democratic and fundamental rights of an increasingly wider section of the population are under threat. The economy is in a mess and corruption, nepotism and crime are rampant. Yet, tragically, the government enjoys support among the Sinhala majority, purely on the strength of a string of military successes. The popularity of the war has also affected the UNP which has gradually shifted its position to appear that it endorses the war without qualification. Thus, substituting one president with another or one chauvinistic government with another cannot resolve the national question or the increasingly worrying plight of democracy and human rights in Sri Lanka.

Therefore, to find a way out of the current crisis, it is important to understand the approaches of the important players to the national question as well as to broader political issues that can no more be separated from the national question. The next section identifies the players in terms of the social group interests that they seek to represent, their ideology, and approach to the national question. The respective roles of important external players are also identified and commented upon.

5

The Scene, the Players, Ideology and Approach

The Present Situation. The conflict escalated rapidly under President Rajapaksha and, between April 2006 and April 2007 alone, over 4000 have been killed, mostly civilians. The number killed since then is likely to be much bigger. Media access to the war zone has been denied since April 2008 and casualty figures have not been released by the government since around September 2008. As said earlier, the LTTE following its retreat from the East has switched to guerrilla attacks there. Whether the LTTE will be forced to abandon positional warfare against the armed forces in the North, go underground and resort to guerrilla warfare is uncertain.

The main opposition party which was briefly emboldened by the surprise land, sea and air attacks by the LTTE in 2007 to challenge the government's ability to defend the country against the LTTE was, however, reluctant to demand an immediate ceasefire and resumption of negotiations. With the armed forces continuing to make territorial gains, the UNP is passively endorsing the pursuit of the war. The government, still far from accomplishing essential tsunami relief work especially in the North-East and unable to handle the refugee problems from the past, has now saddled itself with a burgeoning refugee problem in the North, about which it seems to be cynically indifferent.

The Tamils in the North have since last August faced shortages of essential goods and high prices owing to the closure of the A-9 highway (the main supply route which was opened in 2002 following the CFA and closed in 2006) amid difficult living conditions caused by war-imposed restrictions on cultivation and fishing. Their problems, including matters of personal safety in the army-controlled areas, have been further aggravated by the escalation of the conflict in the North.

In the East, what was a fairly successful agricultural economy of the Tamils even under conditions of war and a reduction in the area under cultivation is in disarray. The means of livelihood for the hundreds of thousand persons displaced internally by war have not been adequately restored and resumption of normal life is not likely with extortion, abductions, killings and other crimes on the rise. This situation has grave implications for the solution to the national question; and, given the dominance of narrow nationalism and opportunist politics, it could aggravate tensions between local communities. The Muslims in the East, who earlier protested about harassment by the LTTE, now, especially since the tsunami, face increased harassment from Sinhala chauvinists, sections of the armed forces, the Special Task Force (STF), and pro-government Tamil paramilitaries. A recent call by the leader of the SLMC asking minority nationalities to unite against chauvinistic oppression echoes these concerns.

The false sense of well being created by the liberalised trade and indiscriminate borrowing from international funding agencies, supplemented by remittances by a migrant worker population (over one and a quarter million adults from a country of twenty million) is now gone. The rising crime rate, child labour and child abuse, drug addiction, prostitution, rising unemployment amid migration of skilled labour for overseas employment, decline in social values, wrecking of family life owing to one or both parents seeking jobs abroad are among the many social ills that are directly related to the open economic policy adopted in 1978. The war which has added to the economic and social ills has also been the pretext to sell many successful state ventures to local and foreign 'investors', to be asset-stripped and abandoned, or for plunder by businesses looking for short term profit. Covert undermining of the role of the state in the public sector and social services, under pressure from the IMF has further burdened the people, and the political and economic instability have affected foreign investment as well as tourism-related income and employment.

A breed of new rich with wealth of dubious origins has emerged, and alongside it an underworld on which the rich and the leading political parties rely for their safety and survival, while exposing the society at large to unwanted risks.

It is long since the mechanisms for the enforcement of law and delivery of justice became politicised. Today, the country is fast drifting towards state-engineered chaos with routine unlawful killings, kidnapping and 'disappearing'. The law and order arm of the state is indifferent if not involved. Harassment of Sinhalese journalists and politicians directly and indirectly by the state was on the decline since around 1992 but has risen steeply in the past two years. There is fear that the country is heading towards an authoritarian state with the armed forces and the underworld working together to keep all political opposition at bay. The Presidential ruling of 23.4.2007 authorising the armed forces to carry out the duties of the police is yet to be implemented, but not a good sign.

Thus it is becoming increasingly difficult to isolate the solution of the national question from the issues of democratic and human rights and struggles against imperialist globalisation and foreign domination. Hence the positions of the various players towards the national question have to be seen in the context of their class loyalties as well as their attitude to imperialism.

Sinhala Nationalism: the Shades of Chauvinism. At the core of Sinhala nationalist ideology is the notion that the Sinhalese (or Sinhala Buddhists to some) are the true sons of the soil. This assumption has been readily extended to deny other ethnic groups equality with the Sinhalese. The UNP has been the main Sinhala bourgeois political party, with pro-imperialist trappings, followed by the SLFP, which for over a quarter century, identified itself with the national bourgeois interests and adopted, within limits, a social reformist and anti-imperialist programme. However, since the weakening of the

SLFP by its electoral defeat in 1977 and the adoption of the liberal economic policy in 1978, the difference in substance between the two parties on matters such as globalisation, liberalisation and privatisation did not take long to fade into insignificance, except for the occasional ritual denunciation of foreign domination by the odd SLFP politician.

Neither the UNP nor the SLFP recognised the Tamils, let alone the other ethnic groups, as a nationality but were compelled by force of circumstances to accept the existence of traditional Tamil homelands and the right of the Tamils to some form of autonomy. The position on the degree of autonomy was not always consistent and both parties have, under pressure from extreme chauvinists and often without resistance, abandoned their own proposals for regional self-government for the Tamils. Also, the two parties have used issues concerning the Tamils for political gain, promoted chauvinist politics for electoral advantage, and obstructed moves to solve the national question by the rival party in power. This attitude still persists.

Neither party has voluntarily sought a solution to the national question, and it is unlikely that, as long as the bourgeois parliamentary political system is in place, they will, in the absence of mass political pressure or, as in the case of the Indo-Sri Lanka Accord, pressure from a dominant foreign power, consent to a solution to the national question based on the recognition of the rights of the nationalities and ethnic groups. Even when agreement has been reached, the temptation has been strong to cheat or to go back on what was agreed, as seen in the de-merging of the Northern and Eastern Provinces in 2007.

It is important to note that, since the start of the war, neither party sincerely sought a negotiated solution or criticised the excesses of the armed forces. Nor has either denounced chauvinism or campaigned for autonomy for the Tamils as a right rather than a price to pay for peace. Successive governments have been party to institutionalised falsification of history and promotion of chauvinism wherever possible. No step has been taken to end discrimination against minorities, to rectify injustices in the fields of education and employment, or restore language and legal rights of the minority nationalities, which are matters that need not wait for a negotiated settlement of the national question.

The fanatical fringe of Sinhala Buddhist nationalism has nurtured chauvinist ideology besides whipping up communal tension. It was never a major political force although it always had capable spokespersons, some of whom SWRD Bandaranaike accommodated in his grand alliance (the *pancha maha balavegaya,* the front of five forces) in 1956. Successive governments acted to placate Sinhala Buddhist chauvinism in various ways in their bid to keep the Sinhala Buddhist electorate with them. The extreme Sinhala Buddhist groups have effectively lobbied at various levels to canvass opinion against any apparent concession to the minorities. A section, with a strong base among the educated urban upper middle classes, entered electoral politics for the first time as Sihala Urumaya (now renamed JHU) in the year 2001 to secure just one seat on the basis of the total national vote. In the Elections of 2004, it fielded members of the Buddhist clergy as candidates, and the gimmick paid off with voters who were disgusted with corrupt politicians. Despite public disillusion with the conduct of the JHU MPs in parliament, the JHU remains an influential opponent of negotiations with the LTTE and solutions based on any kind of autonomy for the Tamils. Its anti-Tamil and occasional anti-Muslim outbursts are backed by various front organisations and individuals with influence in the media. Although sharing the same class support base as the UNP, the saffron-clad JHU MPs were readily tempted by the perks of office to make a deal with Mahinda Rajapaksha and support him in his bid for presidency in December 2005. The JHU and the JVP encouraged Rajapaksha to take a hard line against the LTTE, and following the cross-over by UNP MPs to the PA in large numbers in 2006-2007, the JHU enabled the fanatically Sinhala Buddhist Champika Ranawaka to become MP and join the Cabinet.

Although the roots of the early leaders of the JVP were in the two factions of the Communist Party, the JVP always had a weakness for chauvinism. Until after its failed insurrection of April 1971 it was hostile to the organised working class; and a part of its programme was the expulsion of the Hill Country Tamils from Sri Lanka. It used Marxist Leninist and Che Guevaraist labels up to 1971; and on re-emergence in 1978 acquired a 'legitimate' Trotskyite label from one of the Fourth Internationals, which withdrew its recognition early this decade in view of the openly chauvinist line of the JVP.

The JVP's interest in the minority nationalities does not go beyond tokenism of the kind practiced by the BJP in India and the right wing parties in the US and the UK. From 1982, the position of the JVP on the national question has been explicitly chauvinistic and opposed to any form of devolution or recognition of traditional Tamil homelands, something that even the UNP and the SLFP had conceded out of political expediency at various times, while acting to deny the Tamils a contiguous territory by colonisation and military occupation. The JVP's compromise with Sinhala Buddhism was consummated by its leaders falling at the feet of the Buddhist *mahanayaka* priests and submitting the JVP manifesto to them for approval on the eve of the parliamentary elections in 2000.

The groups that splintered from the JVP before the 1971 insurrection, for ideological or other reasons, became ineffective but remained Sinhala chauvinist. Splits after the insurrection led, however, to groups that have been free of chauvinist ideology, but unable to organise as political parties.

The opportunist alliance of the JVP with the SLFP exacted its price when the JVP thought it opportune to distance itself from the government in 2007. It received a terrible blow when the government induced a third of the JVP MPs to break away and found the Jathika Nidahas Peramuna, which in all but name is an appendage of the ruling alliance, and targeting the JVP. The JVP remains captive to its unqualified endorsement of the war.

Another overtly chauvinistic group with a 'left' label is the MEP, with origins in the LSSP and a chequered political past. It lost all credibility as a left party when it joined the UNP-led government in 1965. It now relies on an alliance with the SLFP to secure parliamentary seats, and is hostile to peace negotiations with the LTTE and opposes autonomy for the Tamils.

The Buddhist Clergy. The Buddhist clergy is now almost exclusively identified with Sinhala Buddhist chauvinism, although there are still some progressive clergymen. It may surprise many that once several monks were activists and leading members of the left movement and that the Communist Party had among its founders the learned Sri Sumamgala Thera. With the upward mobility of the Buddhist clergy owing to support by the state, wealthy individuals and Buddhist organisations, the clergy, although divided along political, caste and regional lines, act as a privileged social group, and play an important role in carrying forward the cause of Sinhala Buddhism in all major Sinhala nationalist parties. The *mahasanghas* have been given prominence by successive governments and have generally served to obstruct solutions to the national question based on devolution of power.

Tamil Nationalism: Moderates and Militants. The 1980s saw the emergence of young Tamil militants as a political force. But rather than develop into mass political organisations they became armed groups claiming to fight the Tamil national cause with the support but not participation of the Tamil community. Without exception, the main Tamil militant organisations have been petit bourgeois in outlook; and, irrespective of claims to be leftist or radical, they were driven by Tamil nationalism. The prospects for a mass struggle led by a united front of Tamil militant movements were always bleak despite occasional co-operation among cadres of different organisations. Competition for dominance intensified with rising hopes of early success leading to a separate state, a dream encouraged by their Indian patrons, while desire for personal power led to splits and brutal elimination of rivals and, when India imposed its solution on them in 1987, the divisions were too deep to be plastered over.

Although some militant organisations liked to be identified as leftist or even Marxist, in practice their nationalism got the better of their left inclination if any. The desire to acquire a left label was to a considerable extent due to the impact of the success of the mass campaign against caste oppression and untouchability between 1966 and 1971, led by the Marxist Leninists. Although the militants were inspired by the armed resistance of the oppressed castes, they failed to learn the need for democracy, mass participation, mass struggle and above all guidance by sound theoretical principles based on social practice.

The shallowness of the commitment of the Tamil militant organisations and their various factions to the cause of Tamil Eelam became clear when, in the face of impending LTTE domination, they jettisoned their struggle. Some, like the PLOTE and the EPDP, besides siding with the government let their members fight alongside the armed forces of the government in attacks against the LTTE as well as the Tamil people. While this is seen as treachery by many, the reality is that the leading militant groups were saddled with a large membership, acquired when things went well for them; with a sudden change in fortunes and the LTTE monopolising Tamil political affairs in the North East, survival meant either assimilation to the LTTE or seeking the patronage of the Sri Lankan government or their erstwhile handlers in India. The two factions of the TMVP too are close collaborators with the government and the Sri Lankan Army.

EROS (Balakumar faction) was absorbed into the LTTE while the rival faction that supported the government is virtually defunct. The EPRLF (Pathmanabha faction) is an openly pro-Indian group and a weaker faction loyal to Varatharajapperumal, the former Chief Minister of the North-East Province is fully under Indian control. The TULF, ACTC and the former militant groups TELO and EPRLF (Suresh faction), with the blessings of the LTTE, formed the Tamil National Alliance (TNA) to contest parliamentary and other elections to curtail the parliamentary strength of the pro-government EPDP. Splits occurred in this alliance owing to personality clashes as well as issues arising from divided loyalty between the LTTE and the Indian establishment. The TNA successfully contested the last general election under the FP banner to avoid legal embarrassment but has been inadequate in its role as the elected representative of the Tamils. To add to its woes, despite its sworn trust in India, it has been repeatedly humiliated by the Indian government, which prefers more subservient clients even without parliamentary representation.

The LTTE remains the only Tamil nationalist organisation waging armed struggle against the state and, with the Tamil masses being the target of state oppression and war, it is seen by many Tamils as their sole protector. While the LTTE has demonstrated great discipline and capability on the military side and a strong sense of commitment to Tamil liberation, it is lacking in ideology. It should, however, be noted that, it showed remarkable maturity during the peace negotiations to indicate willingness to consider a federal solution based on 'internal' self-determination.

The LTTE is not a leftist organisation, although its cadre and support base comprises the most oppressed sections of the Tamils in the North East, especially since the middle classes fled the country following the intensification of the war. On the political front, excessive emphasis on Tamil national unity resulted in scant attention being paid to internal contradictions concerning class, caste, region and gender. The LTTE is also wavering about globalisation and liberalisation and has avoided confrontation with the US in these matters. The failure of the LTTE in this respect could be traced to the tendency of Tamil nationalism to distance itself from struggles for social justice in the South as well from anti-imperialist campaigns. This is indicative of the considerable influence that the Tamil elite classes continue to have on the LTTE. In recent years, the LTTE, perhaps for tactical reasons, has refrained from criticising the Indian establishment, despite the latter's hegemonic ambitions harming the struggle for Tamil liberation.

There has for long been resentment about taxation by the LTTE, especially among Muslim traders and cultivators in the East, and that has contributed to ethnic tension. The LTTE has been most severely, and deservingly, criticised for its intolerance to political dissent. Many of the faults of the LTTE in issues of human and democratic rights, restriction of freedom of expression and movement, and on political activity arise from the reliance of the LTTE mainly on armed struggle rather than broad-based mass struggle with armed struggle as an essential component. The lack of discussion and debate among the masses and the LTTE's claim to be the sole representative of the Tamils have obstructed the democratisation of the struggle, the formation of a broad united front to confront the oppressive state, and uniting with other victims of state and imperialist oppression.

The LTTE, like other militant organisations, had seen splits but none more damaging than the one in 2004 leading to the formation of the TMVP. The TMVP has the benefit of regional sentiments in the East, especially among the Tamil middle class; but the credibility of the now deeply divided TMVP is poor as a liberation movement. The prospects of the TMVP becoming a significant political force are hindered by the government and the armed forces playing Karuna against Pillayan. The conflict in the TMVP will deepen and the probable outcome will be that both factions will be restricted to playing roles akin to that of the EPDP, but with the added complexity of conflicts with the Muslims.

Muslims: New Awareness and Old Tactics. The Muslims, while sharing a common language with the Tamils, maintained a separate identity and began to assert it early in the 20th century. The demography of the Muslims determined, however, that Muslim nationalism could not express itself in ways similar to Tamil nationalism. Survival demanded a stable relationship with the communities amid whom the Muslims lived. Given the difference in nature of the problems faced by the Muslims in different parts of the country no Muslim leadership emerged that could claim to represent the interests of Muslims across the country.

Under the constitution of 1978, the method of election to parliament was changed from the 'first past the post' in the electorate to a proportionate system based on votes secured by political parties in each district. This relieved the Muslim leaders in the North-East of their earlier dependence on the support of a Tamil nationalist party to be elected to parliament. The Muslims were also able to demand better representation from the main parties with whom they aligned in the South. The Sri

Lanka Muslim Congress (SLMC), founded in the 1980s in response to Tamil domination in the East, became a significant political force that performed well in the 1989 general election and won an overwhelming mandate from the Muslims of the East in 1994, to which it held on until the party was ripped apart in late 2000 by dissent based on personal rivalries following the death of its founder leader AHM Ashraff. The SLMC leadership used its parliamentary strength to bargain for cabinet posts and other favours, and compromised its position as a fighter for the rights of the Muslims in the North East. Ashraff set up the SLMC-dominated National Unity Alliance (NUA) in early 2000 in a bid to increase the say of the SLMC in national politics; but the NUA failed to achieve the purpose while the SLMC earned the wrath of the Muslim leaders in the South.

The Muslims in the North-East have good reason for concern about Tamil domination. The political insensitivity of the Tamil militants and their use of violence against 'un-cooperative' Muslims led to the loss of the considerable support and general sympathy that the militants enjoyed among the Muslims up to the mid-1980s. The expulsion of the Muslims from the North by the LTTE in 1990 was a cruel act that did irreparable damage to Tamil-Muslim relationship. Since the mid-1980s, successive governments have systematically manipulated Tamil-Muslim contradictions to their advantage, and mischievous elements among the Muslims, including Home Guards recruited and armed by the government and backed by the armed forces, indulged in acts of violence against Tamils.

The Muslim leaders in the North-East are aware that in the medium and long term the main threat to the Muslims is Sinhala chauvinism, but their opportunism has made them emphasise the contradiction with the Tamils. Thus the demand for a Muslim autonomous region in the East has come up only when the Tamil demand for autonomy in the North-East or the merging of the North-East is discussed. As a result, the demand fails to sound like a genuine, sustained demand for autonomy by the Muslims; and the just demand for autonomy, unfairly, acquires an anti-Tamil hue. Conflicts with Sinhala chauvinists in the East in recent years have further heightened awareness of the chauvinist threat but it will take some time for a comprehensive strategy for the liberation of the Muslim nationality to emerge.

The demography of the Muslims in the South does not permit a Muslim parliamentary political party to represent them and for opportunistic reasons the Muslim leaders are allied to one or another chauvinist party. Abuse of privilege by Muslim parliamentary politicians has often been at the expense of Tamils and Sinhalese and has contributed to the worsening of a delicate relationship between the Muslims and other nationalities.

The failure of the SLMC, its warring factions and rivals in the North East, and the Muslim leaders of the South to address seriously the concerns of the Muslims, the impact of international events comprising the imperialist persecution of the Muslims, and the global upsurge in Islamic fundamentalism and militancy have together contributed to the growth of Islamic fundamentalism in Sri Lanka. While the fundamentalists are divided and politically weak, they have strengthened the place of Islam in the identity of the community and in cultural matters, including the demand on Muslim women to follow the 'Islamic' dress code.

What is sad is the lack of vision on the part of the Muslim leadership and its inability to put forward programmes for the autonomy of the Muslims as a nationality, taking into account the problems faced by the Muslim nationality in the different parts of the island. This lack of vision is evident from the fact that a comprehensive proposal for self-determination for the Muslims first came from the Marxist Leninist NDP, and not any Muslim political party.

Some newly emerged Muslim nationalist groups talk of an Islamic nation in the North-East for which they demand self-determination. Their approach puts at risk the unity and identity of the Muslims as a nationality. The risk is compounded by the prospect of a sizeable Sinhala-speaking Muslim community emerging in the decades to come, as an increasing number of Muslims in the South for various reasons are opting for Sinhala rather than Tamil as their medium of instruction in school.

Since the Sinhala-Buddhist nationalists perceive the national question at best as a conflict between the Sinhalese and the Tamils and more commonly as a terrorist problem, the Muslims do not fare as a part of the national question. They are, however, useful to the extent that they can be used to weaken Tamil claims to a merged North-East as a basis for solving the national question. Thus the Muslim bid for an autonomous region in the East is considered favourably by the UNP and the SLFP while the JVP and the JHU oppose any form of devolution on an ethnic basis.

The Tamil nationalists, on the other hand, have found it hard to digest the fact that the Muslims are a distinct ethnic group. It is only recently that some of the Tamil nationalist parties, for pragmatic reasons, conceded that the Muslims have a distinct identity and a right to autonomy. However, the Tamil nationalist leadership, both moderate and militant, has to this day failed to find common cause with other oppressed nationalities or to put forward proposals that address the national question as a whole.

The Hill Country Tamils. The Hill Country Tamils were alienated from the mainstream of Sri Lankan politics following their disenfranchisement in 1948. This made it possible for the CWC to take advantage of the backwardness of the community and exercise virtual monopoly over the trade unions in the tea plantations. Although the left, especially the Marxist Leninists, made considerable headway in building a politicised trade union movement, that trend met with setbacks in the 1970s.

Corruption and opportunism in the CWC led to dissent and desertions but not to a serious challenge until the Hill Country People's Front (Malaiyaka Makkal Munnani or the MMM) was formed in the early 1990s. With the restoration of the citizenship to the Hill Country Tamils resident in the country, electoral politics and political bargaining for posts and portfolios and various privileges have rendered the CWC and the MMM incapable of fighting the cause of the Hill Country

Tamils, whether it be a demand for a fair minimum wage or a struggle against chauvinistic aggression.

The CWC and the MMM once successfully used ethnic identity as a political issue to shunt out political rivals who accommodate other nationalities, while avoiding struggles to defend the interests of the Hill Country Tamils. Frustration with the leadership of the CWC and the MMM has led to splits and factions in both parties, but for opportunistic reasons. Frustration with the CWC has for some time been a cause for attraction of a section of the youth towards the LTTE, and the MMM sought to use it to its advantage by appearing to be a close ally of the LTTE; but the show was given away when MMM, like the CWC, became a partner in a government that is waging an undeclared war against the LTTE. Elections to the local authorities in 2006 showed that the electoral bases of the CWC and the MMM had eroded considerably, but without an effective alternative. The newly emergent educated youth from the community, guided by genuine left and progressive forces, have taken the initiative to launch struggles for the educational, land and other rights of the Hill Country Tamils. This has exposed the betrayal by the CWC and the MMM, seeking to protect their cabinet posts and business interests. Although the Hill Country Tamils are conscious of the exploitation, discrimination and denial of fundamental rights that they suffer, and of the opportunism of their trade union and political leaders, their awareness needs to crystallise as a political alternative before they can be mobilised to struggle for their rights as a nationality.

The Left: the Old and the New. The parliamentary left paid the price for its opportunism sooner than expected. The commitment of the LSSP and CP to the parliamentary path meant that their humiliation in their election of 1977 destroyed their credibility as a political force, and their alliance with the SLFP denied them an independent political existence as well as eroded their left credentials. The LSSP and the CP have at times distanced themselves from the chauvinistic line of the SLFP, as for example on the Indo-Sri Lanka Accord of 1987, but, as partners in government, they could not dissociate themselves from government policy and its pursuit of war.

The split in the LSSP following its decision to enter into an alliance with the SLFP in 1964 led to the emergence of several Trotskyite groups, but none with a mass political base. The NSSP which originated as a faction in the LSSP in the early 1970s established itself as a political party of considerable strength in the late 1970s. Soon after, splits, more of a personal nature, weakened the NSSP. The NSSP (now known as the Left Front, LF), the United Socialist Party (USP) and the Democratic Left Front (DLF) are products of the fragmentation.

The Marxist Leninists, who broke off with the pro-Soviet CP following a debate between the parliamentary pacifist and the revolutionary lines, underwent splits which did not hurt the revolutionary Communist Party until 1972, when a split was forced by a group of pro-SLFP elements in the wake of the JVP insurrection. That split hurt the party and its working class base, but the splitters soon disintegrated and lost their political identity. A debate on the stand of the party leadership on the Tamil national question led in 1978 to the formation of the Sri Lanka Communist Party (Left), renamed the NDP in 1991, which, although active mainly among the Tamils and the Hill Country Tamils is the strongest Marxist Leninist organisation in the country. There are also the rump of the revolutionary Communist Party, renamed the Maoist Communist Party of Sri Lanka (MCP), and other Marxist Leninist groups and factions in the South, some with roots in the JVP of the 1970s.

A positive development in the left movement since its downfall in the 1970s was the founding of the New Left Front comprising the NSSP, NDP, the United Socialist Party (USP) and three other left groups. It made an impact in the elections to the Provincial Council in 1999, but the opportunism of the leadership of the NSSP in making a deal with the JVP without consulting other members of the NLF led to the break-up of the NLF in 2001. The NSSP adopted the name NLF (now LF). Subsequent attempts to build a united front have been fruitless except for electoral alliances and joint campaigns with specific goals. It appears that the left, especially in the South, has much to learn about broad-based united fronts, common programmes, and unity and struggle within a united front. A section of it still harbours illusions about parliamentary political power, so that electoral alliances take precedence over alliances for mass struggle, while another section has degenerated and become dependent on NGO handouts.

The position of the left on the national question ranges from nominal rejection of chauvinism by the parliamentary left to a demand for autonomy for the Tamils by for example the DLF, and the recognition of the right of the Tamils to self-determination by the NDP, NSSP, USP, the Revolutionary Socialist Party (RSP) and the MCP among others. The attitude towards the LTTE varies: the two parliamentary left parties reject it as terrorist while the DLF is qualified in its criticism of the LTTE; and the NSSP, the MCP and a few others endorse it almost uncritically. The NDP is guarded in its approach: it recognises the LTTE as the effective fighting force of the Tamil nationality but is unreservedly critical of its failings including a lack of democracy, absence of an anti-imperialist stand, and over-emphasis of military aspects over mass participation and mass struggle.

The left traditionally viewed the national question as one concerning the Sinhala and Tamil nationalities, based on the way in which the national question emerged since the 1930s and therefore missed its other less visible but important dimensions. This approach still prevails even among left parties that accept the right of nationalities to self determination. As a result the stand taken by most of the left parties on issues that arise in the course of development of the national crisis has tended to be pragmatic or empirical.

The NDP has, in this respect, made pioneering contributions to the understanding of the national question by examining it historically and dialectically and by drawing on international experience. It has thus been able to advance the concept of the right to self-determination in a way that it could be extended to nationalities without a contiguous territory as well as to ethnic groups with no clearly defined territories to call their own.

The Media. The overall contribution of the mainstream media on the national question has been negative. The Tamil and Sinhala press have in general catered to the interests of the linguistic groups and, except for left and progressive liberal intervention, the contribution of the press to the betterment of ethnic understanding has at best been muted. With the aggravation of the national question, rival newspapers have competed to capture readers among the increasingly nationalistic middle classes.

The radio has been a state monopoly until the 1990s; television entered the scene around 1980 as a state monopoly with the private sector entering the scene in the early 90s. The private sector has tended to be pro-UNP in the past, but amenable to state pressure since the escalation of the national conflict. The state-controlled media has lost credibility over the past few years, thanks to politically appointed administrators and meddling by ruling party politicians.

The Sinhala and English media increasingly cater to Sinhala-Buddhist nationalism, at times serving up vicious chauvinism and wilful distortion of facts, the most notorious being the Island and its sister papers. The Daily Mirror, reputed to be a little fairer in its reporting on the national question, came under threat from those in power in 2007 for reporting serious acts of injustice to the Tamils, and seems to be yielding. Its sister papers compete for the Sinhala Buddhist market. The Tamil newspapers, except for the state-controlled Thinakaran with a poor circulation, give the news a pro-LTTE slant within the permissible limits of pressure from the state and paramilitary forces loyal to it. Although the Thinakaran caters to some extent to the Muslim reader, Muslim opinion is poorly represented in the mainstream media.

The Sinhala newspapers are selective in reporting stories from the Tamil media in ways that are hostile to the Tamil national struggle, and Tamil newspapers give prominence to stories in Sinhala with chauvinistic overtones. There are, however, a few Sinhala and English newspapers that tend to be critical of the way the government handles the national question, but cautious not to appear to be overly sympathetic to the Tamil cause. Their circulation is low and inadequate to counter the impact of the mainstream media

The media, especially Tamil newspapers, were a target of state-sponsored terror in the 1980s, and continue to be under pressure. Attacks on journalists have increased in the past few years to include Sinhala publishers and journalists. Those who reject chauvinism are branded Media Tigers and threatened by chauvinists and harassed by the state. Members of the state-controlled media too have been attacked when loyalty and support to the government was in doubt. Besides, the government is currently working on legislation to curb radio and TV stations, and its implications for democracy, let alone freedom of the media, are frightening.

The Tamil and Sinhala Émigré Communities. Since an overwhelming number of the Sri Lankan Tamils who emigrated fled the country as refugees, many having witnessed the holocaust of 1983, the Tamil nationalist cause finds strong support among them. However, competition for loyalty and demand for financial support for liberation movements followed the Tamils wherever they went. Although a good many Tamils would willingly support the armed struggle of the LTTE, there have been many instances of systematic coercion. That together with intimidation of rival political groups and attempts to suppress critical opinion, which were there even before the LTTE became the dominant player, haunts the Tamil community as well as the support for the struggle.

The Tamil Diaspora, despite its strong feelings about the plight of the Tamils in Sri Lanka and the need for struggle, remains politically backward so that not only the supporters of the LTTE but also its opponents are narrow in their outlook. The narrowness also reflects in the failure of the Tamil community to identify itself with other refugee communities facing oppression in their countries of refuge.

The Sinhala émigré community like its Tamil counterpart was initially based mainly in the UK. It spread to the US, Canada and Australia following the emigration of professionals and skilled personnel that started in the 1970s. The opening up of the economy and the tourism industry in Sri Lanka led to migration to other parts of Europe and the Far East, but in smaller numbers. The violence of 1987-89 led to a large number of Sinhalese leaving to various destinations in Europe. The émigré Sinhala community has become increasingly chauvinistic in ways matching the developments in the country. Today the bulk of the community acts as an active Sinhala nationalist lobby against 'Tamil terrorism'.

The healthy interaction that existed even into the 1970s between the two émigré communities comprising mainly an English-educated middle class has almost ceased to be. That advantage has been lost following the transformation of the national contradiction into war, and even festive occasions that brought the two groups together are now almost segregated.

The 'International Community'. It is cften forgotten that imperialism encourages conflict between communities and has been the agent of war in many Third World countries. The role of imperialism in national conflicts depends on the political orientation of the government. The national question has been used to destabilise countries whose rulers act counter to imperialist interests; and oppression of minorities has been condoned where it involves a government that is warm towards imperialism.

The 'moderate' Tamil leaders have been well received by US and British imperialists when the country had an SLFP government whose policies were not in the economic or geopolitical interests of imperialism. The relationship was good when the Tamil leaders were partners in power with the UNP. Thus the Tamil leaders deluded themselves that American democracy will find common cause with them in their struggle against Sinhala chauvinist oppression. This together with class loyalties partly explains why the Tamil leaders went out of their way to be hostile towards 'communist' countries in general and China in particular.

Things were destined to change when the UNP came to power in 1977 with an unassailable parliamentary majority. Imperialism found in the UNP regime, which lasted until 1994, a strong partner to deliver its plans for Sri Lanka in carrying forward imperialist globalisation. The aggravation of the national question helped to distract public attention from serious economic problems and, once the embarrassment caused by the pogrom of 1983 faded from international memory, imperialism openly backed the war efforts of the UNP government. Support for the government's war efforts has survived to this day, although by the late 1990s peace and stability became desirable for carrying the imperialist agenda further forward.

The US along with Israel has been the biggest supporter of the Sri Lankan military effort by providing military training, arms, information and logistic support. The US banned the LTTE in 1997 and followed it up with pressure on both the government and the LTTE to pursue peace. The '9/11' attack provided the pretext for the US 'War on Terrorism' and for the exertion of further pressure on both the Sri Lankan government and the LTTE to negotiate. Norway, which delivered the goods for the US-sponsored talks between Israel and the PLO, was again the agent. Moves initiated under the PA government bore fruit as soon as the UNP, which was more amenable to the US establishment, formed the government in 2002.

Several US government spokespersons have refused to recognise traditional Tamil homelands and the US has given greater priority to disarming the LTTE than to solving the national question on an equitable basis. The role of the US in causing a split in the LTTE in 2004 was part of a plan to weaken the LTTE militarily.

Although the European community and Japan are not as openly hostile to the LTTE as the US, their position on the national question is dubious. The LTTE and Tamil nationalists who pinned their hopes on Europe to defend the Tamils against state oppression were in for a rude shock when the EU banned the LTTE in 2006 amid a marked rise in attacks on Tamil civilians by the armed forces of the government. Notably, the 'international community', whose response to a whole year of bombing and shelling of the Tamil areas by the Sri Lankan armed forces starting in April 2006 was at most an expression of concern, has been more forthcoming with its criticism of the LTTE for its acts of terror.

The Sri Lankan government's response to statements of concern by the 'International Community' about human rights in Sri Lanka has been either a denial of any wrongdoing or crude abuse of those making the complaints. The 'International Community' does not seem affected by Sri Lanka's conduct or its moves like warming up to Iran, which in other circumstances would have been seen as provocative. The attitude of the 'international community' is best understood in the context of its imperialist agenda and the place for Sri Lanka in it – something that the Sri Lankan government seems to understand very well.

Direct US interest in Sri Lanka has been more strategic than economic. The US has eyed Sri Lanka since the British naval and air bases were closed down in 1957. Attempts to gain a foothold in the country were initiated during the UNP rule from 1965 to 1970 and intensified after the landslide victory of the UNP in 1977. Sri Lanka is important to the US for two purposes: domination over South Asia; and plans to encircle China. US efforts to gain control over the Trincomalee Harbour around 1980 were thwarted by India. US interests in the country were, however, revived around the turn of the century and several military agreements have been signed, the most recent being the Acquisition and Cross-Servicing Agreement signed in March 2007, without protest from India. Today the US has increased its naval presence around Sri Lanka, and has a relay station in Sri Lanka for the Voice of America and other US political broadcasts for South Asia.

Sri Lanka also constitutes an important part of the US plans to implement imperialist globalisation in South Asia, and successive Sri Lankan governments since 1977 have been submissive to the US in this respect. A Free Trade Zone (FTZ) was set up in 1979 close to the international airport as part of the open economic policy, and investors from the Far East moved in fast to take advantage of various subsidies including tax holidays and concessions, and a labour force deprived of trade union rights by special legislation. Another important attraction besides cheap skilled and semi-skilled labour and tax concessions has been the unused quota for the export of garments from Sri Lanka to the US and Europe. Meantime the World Bank, the IMF and the ADB continue with pressure on the government to implement 'structural reforms' to downgrade the role of the state in providing social services and social security; and the cost of the war has served as an excuse for selling all or part of several state owned enterprises, including the highly profitable national airlines, petroleum and telecommunication companies.

Indian Concerns: Gods with Many Faces. India's South Asian policy has been driven by hegemonic ambitions of the ruling classes from the last days of the British Raj. India's direct involvement in the Sri Lankan conflict was prompted by the shift in Sri Lankan foreign policy from strict non-alignment to a pro-US line under JR Jayawardane from 1977.

India provided military training to Tamil militants since the late 1970s on a modest scale and on a much bigger scale since 1983. Most Tamil nationalists misread Indian intentions and believed that India would help them to liberate Tamil Eelam like it did to liberate Bangladesh from Pakistan over a decade earlier. Although the Indo-Sri Lanka accord of 1987 laid bare Indian intentions, there are still many who like to believe that Indira Gandhi was genuinely for a separate Tamil Eelam while her immature son was easily taken for a ride by JR Jayawardane. Illusions about the Indian ruling establishment continue to be propagated by many Tamil leaders, more out of self-interest than ignorance.

One constraint on India has been the strong sentiments in Tamilnadu about the plight of the Sri Lankan Tamils. The assassination of Rajeev Gandhi, the motivation for which is still very cloudy, as well as the misconduct of renegades from various liberation movements and some negative aspects of the Sri Lankan refugee problem drained the sympathy for the Tamils, with, of course, help from the elitist media, especially *the Hindu* and *Indian Express* groups of newspapers. Attitudes towards the Sri Lankan Tamils have, however, become more sympathetic in the past decade, especially since the resumption of hostilities in the North-East.

The DMK and its leader have been as elusive as ever while

the ADMK leader and the Congress have been uncompromising in their hostility towards the LTTE. It should also be noted that the few friends that the LTTE has like the MDMK and the PMK in Tamilnadu, George Fernandes and, interestingly, Bal Thakeray were, however, of no avail in lifting the ban on the LTTE even when they were partners in the BJP-led government.

The Indian establishment cynically interfered in the peace process in ways that hindered progress, while claiming to keep out of it. It is well known that the Sri Lankan Prime Minister and the Norwegian mediator had debriefing sessions in New Delhi after every round of talks with the LTTE on various issues. The Indian establishment has made it clear that it does not want anyone other than a pliable client in control of affairs in any part of Sri Lanka where India has commercial or strategic interests. It should be noted that, with Indo-US collaboration and collusion much in the open, Indian ambitions for regional hegemony and US ambitions for global domination have become mutually accommodative.

India has several clients among political organisations in Sri Lanka, including the JVP despite its protests abut Indian meddling. It also has influence over important personalities in nearly every political party; and the conduct of the two previous Indian High Commissioners had been compared with that of a Viceroy in the colonial era. Thus, Indian interests will in one way or another continue to play a major role in the resolution or otherwise of the national crisis, based on the interests of Indian capitalism and Indian hegemonic interests.

Indian capital began to penetrate Sri Lanka following the open economic policy. It benefited from the deterioration of the national economy of Sri Lanka and controls a sizeable section of the foreign trade. Although it suffered a brief setback in 1988-89 during the JVP insurrection, it recovered fast to expand into the privatised plantation sector and other major ventures, most significantly the petroleum sector which it has come to dominate since privatisation. India sees in Sri Lanka a good market for its products, especially with growing consumerism and the decline in local production. Collaboration between Sri Lankan and Indian companies in the financial and service sectors also has seen rapid growth in the past decade.

India clearly asserted its hegemonic stand in the Indo-Sri Lanka Accord of 1987, and in 1999 imposed on Sri Lanka an unequal trade agreement whose terms were revised in 2002 to the detriment of Sri Lanka. While India is not in a position to control Sri Lanka militarily, it has been able to restrain Sri Lanka from concluding military agreements with other countries that could challenge Indian hegemony. The Sethusamudram project on which work commenced in 2006 is yet another instance where the Indian state arrogantly ignored Sri Lankan concerns and the Sri Lankan state has abjectly failed to stand up for its people.

Vested interests portray Sri Lanka's friendly relationship with China and Pakistan as inimical to India to make a case for greater Indian involvement in the Sri Lankan national question. Tamil nationalists in Sri Lanka and Tamilnadu have tried to use this argument to persuade India to side with the Sri Lankan Tamils. But the Indian establishment seems to have other ideas. It has applied pressure the Sri Lankan government to purchase its defence equipment from India rather than China or Pakistan, and has provided Sri Lanka with equipment as well as personnel. Pretences to the contrary had to be abandoned when a recent air attack by the LTTE injured Indian technical staff manning a military radar system in northern Sri Lanka.

Soon after, in October 2008, the Communist Party of India initiated a mass protest in Tamilnadu against the Indian government policy on the Sri Lankan national question, and its success alerted the DMK, which also saw in it a way to divert mass attention form the poor performance of the state government. The DMK hijacked the protest with the threat that its MPs will resign en bloc if the Premier failed to persuade Sri Lanka to agree to a ceasefire. What followed was pure theatre, and surprised no one who knew anything of the politics of Tamilnadu.

As evident from the continuing protests there is genuinely strong feeling in Tamilnadu against the war, and it is a good sign that the protesters are increasingly distancing themselves from the stunts of the DMK. However, while the demand for the cessation of Indian military support to Sri Lanka is useful, given India's hegemonic ambitions, the benefit of potential Indian involvement apart from a sincere call for an immediate ceasefire in Sri Lanka is doubtful.

Other Factors. There are vested interests working against an end to the armed conflict and others using the conflict to advance their self-interest. Arms dealers need the continuation of armed conflicts in various parts of the world. Profiteering in the arms trade is not possible without the help of people in influential positions on either of the conflict. Serious charges of corruption have been made against politicians and leading figures in the Sri Lankan defence establishment. Equally there are vested interests among Tamil nationalists who do not want peace. Keenness on the part of certain sections of the media to pursue the war makes one wonder if the arms dealers have cast its net far and wide.

Another group of cynical operators comprises the NGOs. While they appear to be providers of relief to affected masses and campaigners for peace, the local NGOs mainly comprise careerists delivering the agenda of INGOs, most of which are extensions to the arms of imperialist governments. Recent escalation of the conflict has led to the suspension of relief work by NGOs in the war affected areas, and the people, already denied and deprived by the government, have been reduced to a state of helplessness. Thus the NGOs have positioned themselves as a necessary evil in a situation where the government purposely fails its people.

The worst harm done by the NGOs is through handouts, and 'self-help' and 'leadership development' projects, which really make the people less and less self reliant; meanwhile the NGO campaign against political work undermines mass mobilisation with clear political objectives.

The Sri Lankan national question is in many ways less complex than that of many third world countries but has been aggravated by the repeated failure of successive governments to arrest the escalation of the contradictions. The transformation of the national question into a national crisis and war was by design and driven by class interests. Thus its resolution will not be possible without identifying and isolating the forces that work against the interests of the country, its nationalities and ethnic groups, and the toiling masses. In the final analysis the resolution of the national question is interwoven with the struggle for social justice; thus, while endorsing the need for struggle including armed struggle where necessary to overcome chauvinist oppression and war, one should not lose sight of the fact that the national contradiction is not a hostile contradiction and needs to be resolved peacefully while persisting in struggle against the oppressors.

The people of Sri Lanka want peace. Although peace efforts of the past failed to address the national question in its totality and addressed only some manifestations of the problem, there are lessons to learn from the positive and negative aspects of past efforts. The next and concluding section briefly outlines a principled approach for the resolution of the national question and the short- and long-term strategies for its resolution.

6

The Search for a Solution

Well over a hundred thousand lives have been lost as a result of the war; and both the government and the LTTE have tended to underestimate the figures. With more than 300,000 people displaced by ongoing the war in the Vanni, the number of internally displaced is probably between 600,000 and 700,000, comprising mainly Tamils, and including Muslims driven out of the North and Sinhalese affected by war. The Tamil refugee population in Europe, Canada and Australia adds to around 800,000; the number in India fluctuates with the changing situation in Sri Lanka and probably hovers around 150,000. What is important is that, of those killed, a vast majority belong to the impoverished classes comprising peasants, fisher-folk and agricultural labourers; and that those languishing in refugee camps in India and Sri Lanka are also from the same class background.

From the Banda-Chelva Pact of 1958 to the failed peace talks of 2002-2003, efforts to deal with the national question have been matters of expediency rather than addressing the sources of the problem. As a result, any agreement reached is readily scrapped under pressure from interest groups or fails to lead to further action. The latter is best illustrated by the plight of the CFA of 2002: the cessation of hostilities led to complaisance on the part of the UNP government and solving the national question lost priority.

What brought the UNP government and the LTTE to the negotiating table was not love for peace or the realisation that the national question cannot be resolved by war. It was the strain on the economy, the unpopularity of a failed war, and pressure from the US that motivated the government; and it was the depletion of human and material resources, and pressures from a war weary population and from the US and EU that persuaded the LTTE.

The concern of the 'international community' is more about ensuring a climate of peace in which imperialism could take full control of the human and material resources and strategic locations of the country. Thus, going by recent international experience, it is futile to hope that any form of foreign intervention including that of the UN will lead to lasting peace or a fair solution to the national question.

All-party conferences and other such fora have only been delaying devices used by successive governments which have been unwilling to solve the problem. All government proposals thus far fell well short of the aspirations of the Tamil people, and even the report by the Panel of Experts appointed by the President in 2006, whose recommendations were still inadequate but went some way towards addressing some of the major grievances, were discarded by the President in favour of a totally inadequate proposal by his party, the SLFP. Thus it seems that the government has been playing for time in the hope that it will soon weaken the LTTE sufficiently so that a solution which is palatable to the chauvinists could be imposed on the LTTE and the Tamil people. But this approach has only prolonged the war, further ruined the already tottering economy, and caused untold misery to the people.

The war cannot be fought to a finish and neither side can secure absolute victory. Thus it needs to be brought to an end. But the government is able to pursue the war because the Sinhala masses have been conditioned to believe that the war is against terrorism and that the armed forces are winning. They do not know the cost of the war and nobody is asking either. Support for the war could be sustained as long as the armed forces do not suffer major reversals. But even a military victory for the government will not end the armed conflict but lead to a great tragedy for the whole country.

The Short Term. Thus the immediate priority is to bring an end to the conflict and take steps to help the people in the war affected areas to return to 'normal living conditions'. External pressure alone is inadequate for this and could be counterproductive. The immediate need is for a campaign for peace and the restoration of 'normal living conditions'. The solution to the national question is a continuous project that would initially require the establishment and acceptance of basic principles. Implementation cannot be on a rigid basis but evolved in a flexible way on the basis of experience without compromising on basic principles.

Pressure should be brought upon the government and the LTTE through mass campaigns for peace and a political solution to urge cessation of hostilities and initiate negotiations forthwith. Peace talks alone will serve no purpose unless urgent steps are taken to restore normal life in the war affected areas. Mechanisms need to be set up to provide essential services and need to be implemented in the spirit of co-operation. While peace negotiations and matters relating to abiding by ceasefire agreements would necessarily concern the government and the LTTE, work relating to the restoration of normal life would require a leading role for the local communities.

Among immediate priorities are:

1. Cessation of hostilities and withdrawal of all armed personnel from areas with large civilian concentration
2. Reduction in the territory allocated to military camps
3. Resettlement of all internally displaced people in areas of their choice
4. Restoration of the livelihood of the people
5. Rehabilitation of war affected families and individuals and compensation for loss of life and property
6. Restoration of social amenities and services
7. Restoration of freedom of movement for the people and opening of all highways affected by war

It is important that realistic time frames are set for the various phases of the negotiations and the strict implementation of decisions. Two proposals exist that could serve as starting points for determining an interim arrangement for the period of transition to the long term solution. One is the ISGA proposal put forward by the LTTE in 2003 and the other the proposal submitted in 2006 by the Panel of Experts nominated by President Rajapaksha. There is some common ground between the two proposals so that with both parties taking a flexible and conciliatory attitude on matters affecting the well being of the victims of war, it should be possible to arrive at a sensible working arrangement. Popular support and encouragement for the negotiations is essential and the campaign for peace and a political solution should be actively pursued even while the negotiations are in progress, to counteract mischief by vested interests and forces of chauvinism and extremism.

It is, however, essential that the campaign for the restoration of peace and an interim solution to the national question does not lose sight of the role of imperialism and the need to resist imperialism and its attempts to manipulate the national question to serve its agenda of imperialist globalisation.

The bourgeois chauvinist state has already trained its guns against left and progressive forces among the Sinhalese who are opposed to the war, and in the process initiated an onslaught against democratic and human rights. Thus the liberation struggle of the oppressed nationalities should seriously explore possibilities of new alliances, even in the short term, in the struggle against the chauvinist state.

Long term. A just and resilient long term solution to the national question needs to be based on the principle of the right to self-determination. That right cannot be reduced or restricted to be the right to secession but instead be seen as the right of each nationality and ethnic group to determine freely its mode of coexistence with other communities. While the right to self-determination for nationalities with a contiguous territory would readily include the right to secession along with the freedom to determine the form and degree of autonomy that the nationality would have within the union, nationalities and ethnic groups who cannot define a contiguous territory for themselves should enjoy the right to determine the form of autonomy that is appropriate to them.

Autonomous regions and administrative units should be

set up as necessary to protect and develop the socio-cultural identity of an ethnic group and facilitate its educational and economic development. An ethnic group could exercise its choice to decide whether it wants a separate autonomous region or unit for itself or share it with one or several other ethnic groups. This will be of particular advantage to the Muslims and Hill Country Tamils. The Muslims could have predominantly Muslim autonomous regions in the East and autonomous units elsewhere which may be exclusively Muslim or shared with another ethic group. The situation for the Hill Country Tamils will vary with region according to the variation in their population concentration. The approach suggested here will be of particular benefit to national minorities like the Attho whose territory is under constant threat from chauvinism, and give them the opportunity to adapt to the changing environment at their own pace without fear of losing their cultural identity.

The kind of right to self-determination discussed above is unlike 'the right to internal self-determination' adopted by the United Nations some years ago, where the right to self-determination is curtailed to deny the right to secession. Marxist Leninists cannot make the principle of self-determination restrictive and thereby a licence for communities that could be defined as nations or nationalities with a contiguous territory to dominate national minorities.

It is premature to propose any particular model for devolution of power and for the setting up of autonomous regions and units. However, the Soviet Union, China, and Nicaragua under the Sandinistas in the 1980s offer a variety of options; and China and Nicaragua have shown that it is feasible to recognise as national minorities ethnic groups with population in the hundreds and set up autonomous units to defend and develop their ethnic identity. Lenin and Mao Zedong had warned communists about Great Russian chauvinism and Han chauvinism, respectively, and urged communists to be on the guard against such thinking. Nationalism thrives because of oppressive social conditions and will survive as long as such conditions prevail. The challenge before us is to eliminate the conditions that transform what are essentially friendly contradictions among nationalities into hostile contradictions.

To demand that the LTTE should disarm before peace talks or negotiations to resolve the national question is unfair. An oppressed people have the right to defend themselves and armed oppression cannot be met with bare hands. However, there are questions of democratic rights, political freedom and struggles against social injustice within the Tamil community that cannot be lightly brushed aside in the name of unity or as matters that could wait until liberation. On the contrary, democratisation of the struggle and encouragement of political freedom strengthen liberation struggles.

The struggle against chauvinist state oppression will persist until and even after a negotiated settlement, but not necessarily as armed struggle. Armed struggle is an option that a liberation movement does not readily discard. But what is important is to develop other forms of struggle and expand the scope of the struggle by broadening the base of the struggle.

The militarization of the Sri Lankan state entered a new phase after 1983 and several hard won rights and freedoms have been taken away in the name of fighting terrorism. National security should not be allowed to be the pretext for denying democratic and fundamental rights; and if the current trend is not challenged, arrested and reversed, the country will sooner than later come under the jackboots of anti-democratic chauvinists, including the likes of the JHU and the JVP.

One should seriously consider the prospect of the struggle for democratic, human and fundamental rights soon becoming a common cause that will be as important as the struggle against national oppression or even superseding the latter as a struggle against imperialism and local reaction. The task of the left, progressive and democratic forces will then be to bring together the struggles against all forms of oppression and direct them against the local oppressors and their imperialist masters.